# THE LEADER'S HANDBOOK

EDITED BY
## ANDREW POULIN

ARCHWAY
PUBLISHING

Archway Publishing books may be ordered through booksellers or by contacting:

Archway Publishing
1663 Liberty Drive
Bloomington, IN 47403
www.archwaypublishing.com
844-669-3957

ISBN: 978-1-6657-3413-4 (sc)
ISBN: 978-1-6657-3414-1 (hc)
ISBN: 978-1-6657-3415-8 (e)

Library of Congress Control Number: 2022921028

Print information available on the last page.

Archway Publishing rev. date: 06/01/2023

# CONTENTS

Philosophy is no trick to catch the public; it is not devised for show. It is a matter, not of words, but of facts. It is not pursued in order that the day may yield some amusement before it is spent, or that our leisure may be relieved of a tedium that irks us. It molds and constructs the soul; it orders our life, guides our conduct, shows us what we should do and what we should leave undone; it sits at the helm and directs our course as we waver amid uncertainties. Without it, no one can live fearlessly or in peace of mind. Countless things that happen every hour call for advice; and such advice is to be sought in philosophy.[1]

—Seneca

# INTRODUCTION

Leadership is hard. It is a challenging, sometimes lonely, and tough affair. But it is also equally rewarding, impactful, and extremely important. During one particularly challenging leadership moment, I was searching for guidance and pulled out some of my old notebooks on leadership I had kept since high school.

Within these pages I would write down inspiring excerpts gathered from various figures throughout history, including many of the early classical philosophers like Aristotle, Plato, and Socrates, and some of the Stoics like Epictetus and Marcus Aurelius. They thought, wrote, and spoke about issues of critical importance in their daily lives, but also about issues that transcend their time and live on today.

Feeling inspired, I began reading some of these philosophers with a renewed interest and noticed several themes emerge among these early thinkers – themes like character, courage, compassion, humility, justice, communication, judgment, action, resilience, and wisdom – what I now consider the ten core leadership values. However, the more I read, the more I also felt like the wisdom contained in these pages was spread across many resources and just not easily digestible to most people, especially young leaders. This book tries to help bridge that gap.

The ten core leadership values identified in this handbook from the ancient wisdom of these early philosophers will not cover every situation you may encounter as a leader. However, they can help guide you to the best decision and the best outcome for you and your organization.

Philosophy and leadership involve a great deal of reflection. We must reflect to assess our progress towards goals. We must reflect to gauge the success or failure of our teams. But most importantly, we must reflect to ensure we are living in accordance with our values. If we do that, we will empower ourselves and each other to achieve our full potential as leaders.

The ancient words contained in these pages should not be an end, but a starting point. I hope they will bring you the same strength, optimism, and inspiration they brought me.

# AUTHOR'S NOTE

Thank you for reading *The Leader's Handbook*! One quick note before you begin: the language, writing, and translations of many of the early philosophers often spoke from the male perspective. However, the lessons encompassed here apply equally to men and women, and will be valuable to anyone seeking to improve their leadership.

## BOOK 1

# CHARACTER

It is fitting to begin this leadership handbook where we all must start in our very core: with character.

Character is absolutely integral to leadership, and nothing is more important. It defines who you are and is a testament to what you will do when no one is looking. In any organization, whether it's in business, the military, government, the non-profit sector, or elsewhere, you will not be able to reach your maximum effectiveness as a leader unless you have complete, unquestioned character.

The soul is dyed the color of its thoughts. Think only on those things that are in line with your principles and can bear the light of day. The content of your character is your choice. Day by day, what you choose, what you think, and what you do is who you become. Your integrity is your destiny – it is the light that guides your way.[2]

—Heraclitus

> *Day by day, what you choose, what you think, and what you do is who you become.*
>
> - Heraclitus

The human being is born with an inclination toward virtue.[3]

—Musonius Rufus

Good actions give strength to ourselves and inspire good actions in others.[4]

—Plato

If you want to keep your character in line with nature, you have every hope of success, all the means you need, and not a worry in the world. Because if you want to keep what is yours by right and is by nature free – and these are the only things you want – you have nothing to worry about. No one else controls them or can take them away from you. If you want to be a man of honor and a man of your word, who is going to stop you? You say you don't want to be obstructed or forced to do something against your will – well, who is going to force you to desire things that you don't approve, or dislike something against your better judgment?[5]

—Epictetus

> *If you want to be a man of honor and a man of your word, who is going to stop you?*
>
> - Epictetus

Character is destiny.[6]

—Heraclitus

Good character is not formed in a week or a month. It is created little by little, day by day. Protracted and patient effort is needed to develop good character.[7]

—Heraclitus

It seems to me that just as those who do not exercise their bodies cannot carry out their physical duties, so those who do not exercise their characters cannot carry out their moral duties: they can neither do what they ought to do nor avoid what they ought to avoid.[8]

—Xenophon

There are but three kinds of men in the world. The first, when he helps someone out, makes it known that he expects something in return. The second would never be so bold, but in his mind he knows what he has done and considers the other person to be in his debt. The third somehow doesn't realize what he has done, but he's like a vine that bears its fruit and asks for nothing more than the pleasure of producing grapes. A horse gallops, a dog hunts, a bee makes honey, one man helps another, and the vine bears fruit in due season. You ought to be like the third fellow, who does good without giving it a second thought.[9]

—Marcus Aurelius

Naturally there are a lot of things about me requiring to be built up or fined down or eliminated. Even this, the fact that it perceives the failings it was unaware of in itself before, is evidence of a change for the better in one's character.[10]

—Seneca

In bad or corrupted natures the body will often appear to rule over the soul, because they are in an evil and unnatural condition. At all events we may firstly observe in living creatures both a despotical and a constitutional rule; for the soul rules the body with a despotical rule, whereas the intellect rules the appetites with a constitutional and royal rule. And it is clear that the rule of the soul over the body, and of the mind and the rational element over the passionate, is natural and expedient; whereas the equality of the two or the rule of the inferior is always hurtful.[11]

—Aristotle

There are three kinds of states of character to be avoided, namely vice, incontinence and brutishness.[12]

—Aristotle

Where does the good lie?
'In the will.'
And evil?
'Also in the will.'
And things neither good nor bad –
'...lie in whatever is external to the will.'[13]
　　—Epictetus

It is not living, but living well which we ought to consider most important.[14]
　　—Socrates

All human happiness or misery takes the form of action; the end for which we live is a certain kind of activity, not a quality. Character gives us qualities, but it is in our actions--what we do--that we are happy or the reverse--a tragedy is impossible without action, but there may be one without Character.[15]
　　—Aristotle

Come back with your shield – or on it.[16]
　　—Plutarch, relating what Spartan mothers would tell their sons as they departed for battle

Whatever happens, either you have the strength to bear it or you don't. If you have the strength, stop complaining, be grateful, and bear it. If you lack the strength, there is still no reason to lose patience, for once your strength is consumed, the struggle will end. But remember, you have the power within you to endure anything.[17]
　　—Marcus Aurelius

> *You have the power*
> *within you to*
> *endure anything.*
>
> - Marcus Aurelius

Surely every man ought to regard self-discipline as the foundation of moral goodness, and to cultivate it in his character before anything else. Without it, who could either learn anything good or practice it to a degree worth mentioning? Or who could escape degradation both of body and mind if he is a slave to his appetites?[18]

   —Socrates

No man is free who cannot control himself.[19]

   —Pythagoras

Since, while the end is an object of wish, the means to it are objects of deliberation and choice, the actions that are related to the means will be performed in accordance with choice, and voluntarily. But the exercise of moral virtues is related to means. Therefore virtue lies in our power, and similarly so does vice; because where it is in our power to act, it is also in our power not to act, and where we can refuse we can also comply. So if it is in our power to do a thing when it is right, it will also be in our power not to do it when it is wrong; and if it is in our power not to do it when it is right, it will also be in our power not to do it when it is wrong. And if it is in our power to do right and wrong, and similarly not to do them; and if, as we saw, doing right or wrong is the essence of being good or bad, it follows that it is in our power to be decent or worthless.[20]

   —Aristotle

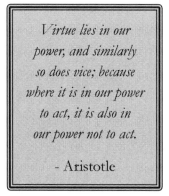

*Virtue lies in our
power, and similarly
so does vice; because
where it is in our power
to act, it is also in
our power not to act.*

- Aristotle

As you are careful when you walk not to step on a nail or turn your ankle, so you should take care not to do any injury to your character at the same time. Exercise such caution whenever we act, and we will perform the act with less risk of injury.[21]
—Epictetus

...There remains only one distinguishing mark of the good man: his love and delight in the thread of his own destiny and his refusal to soil or upset with an orgy of sensations the divine spirit dwelling within him, where a serene peace reigns and God is obeyed and no untrue words are spoken and no unjust deeds performed. Even if everyone else questions his ability to live so simply, modestly, and happily, he doesn't let their doubts disturb him or divert him from the road leading to his life's destination, which he intends to reach pure and peaceful and prepared to take his leave in unforced allegiance to his fate.[22]
—Marcus Aurelius

The character produced from wealth is that of a prosperous fool.[23]
—Aristotle

Here's a thought that should flatten any false pride: it is no longer possible to live your entire life, not even your adult life, as a philosopher. How far short of philosophy you fall is plain to others, as it is to yourself. Your life is flawed, your reputation tainted, and it is no longer possible to win the glory of being a philosopher. Even your calling in life militates against it. Having seen these truths with your own eyes, stop worrying about what others may think and be content to live the rest of your life, as long or short as it may be, according to the requirements of your own nature. Know these requirements well and let nothing pry you from them.

You have searched everywhere, and in all your wanderings you have not found happiness—not in clever arguments nor in wealth, fame, pleasure, or anything else. Where is happiness then? In doing what a man's nature requires. And how will you do this? By basing your actions and desires on sound principles. What principles? Principles that distinguish right from wrong and demonstrate that nothing is good for a man unless it helps him to be just, responsible, courageous, and free, while nothing is bad that fails to produce the opposite result.[24]
—Marcus Aurelius

> *In every sphere of conduct people develop qualities corresponding to the activities they pursue.*
>
> - Aristotle

'Well probably he is the sort of person that doesn't take care.' But people get into this condition through their own fault, by the slackness of their lives; i.e. they make themselves unjust or licentious by behaving dishonestly or spending their time in drinking and other forms of dissipation; for in every sphere of conduct people develop qualities corresponding to the activities that they pursue. This is evident from the example of people training for any competition or undertaking: they spend all their time in exercising. So to be unaware that in every department of conduct moral states are the result of corresponding activities is the mark of a thoroughly imperceptive person.[25]

—Aristotle

Bear in mind that the measure of a man is the worth of the things he cares about.[26]

—Marcus Aurelius

Character is that which reveals moral purpose, exposing the class of things a man chooses and avoids.[27]

—Aristotle

No matter what anyone else does or says, I must be good. [28]

—Marcus Aurelius

Virtue, then, is of two kinds, intellectual and moral. Intellectual virtue owes both its inception and its growth chiefly to instruction and for this very reason needs time and experience. Moral goodness, on the other hand, is the result of habit, from which it has actually got its name, being a slight modification of the word *ethos*.[29]

—Aristotle

Remember that you are an actor in a play, the nature of which is up to the director to decide. If he wants the play to be short, it will be short; if he wants it long, it will be long. And if he casts you as one of the poor, or as a cripple, as a king or as a commoner – whatever role is assigned, the accomplished actor will accept and perform it with impartial skill. But the assignment of roles belongs to another.[30]

    —Epictetus

Every nature finds fulfillment in pursuing the right path. For a nature like yours endowed with reason, this means refusing to approve ideas that are false or foggy, directing your energies only to the common good, limiting your likes and dislikes to those things that lie within your grasp, and rejoicing in everything the universal nature has assigned you.[31]

    —Marcus Aurelius

Moral goodness is enough by itself to create a happy life.[32]

    —Cicero

Be a boxer, not a gladiator, in the way you act on your principles. The gladiator takes up his sword only to put it down again, but the boxer is never without his fist and has only to clench it.[33]

    —Marcus Aurelius

Are my guiding principles healthy and robust? On this hangs everything. The rest, whether I can control it or not, is but smoke and the gray ashes of the dead.[34]

    —Marcus Aurelius

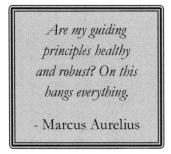

*Are my guiding principles healthy and robust? On this hangs everything.*

- Marcus Aurelius

Consider at what price you sell your integrity; but please, for God's sake, don't sell it cheap.[35]

—Epictetus

This brings me back to moral goodness. It may be held to fall into three subdivisions. The first is the ability to distinguish the truth from falsity, and to understand the relationship between one phenomenon and another and the causes and consequences of each one. The second category is the ability to restrain the passions (*pathe* in Greek) and to make the appetites (*hormai*) amenable to reason. The third, which is relevant here, is the capacity to behave considerately and understandingly in our associations with other people.[36]

—Cicero

For many men value appearances more than reality—thus they violate what's right. Everyone's prepared to sigh over some suffering man, though no sorrow really eats their hearts, or they can pretend to join another person's happiness forcing their faces into smiling masks. But a good man discerns true character—he's not fooled by eyes feigning loyalty, favoring him with watered-down respect.[37]

—Aeschylus

If you want to be good at anything, the shortest, safest and most reputable way is to try to make yourself really good at it. If you consider the virtues that are recognized among human beings, you will find that they are all increased by study and practice.[38]

—Xenophon

Love of honor is the one thing that never grows old, and it is not wealth – as some people say – but honor that brings the most joy amid the frailty of age.[39]

—Pericles

Don't be a Caesar drunk with power and self-importance: it happens all too easily. Keep yourself simple, good, pure, sincere, natural, just, god-fearing, kind, affectionate, and devoted to your duty. Strive to be the man your training in philosophy prepared you to be, Fear God, serve mankind. Life is short; the only good fruit to be harvested in this earthly realm requires a pious disposition and charitable behavior.

In all things, show yourself to be the faithful student of Antoninus, who never tired of living in complete accord with reason, acting with moderation on all occasions, controlling even the expressions on his face. Be worthy of his sweetness and devotion, his indifference to praise, his love of putting things in order. Remember how he never abandoned a subject until he had studied it in depth and understood it thoroughly; how he put up with unjustified accusations without saying a word; how he never acted in haste or listened to slander; how he weighed carefully a man's character and actions; how he was never spiteful, craven, suspicious, or pedantic; how simple were his tastes and spare his needs in lodging and bed and dress and food and service; and how he loved hard work and bore the inconveniences and irritations of life with inexhaustible patience.

O, what a man he was! He could work in one place from morning till night without pausing for nourishment or rest and without relieving himself before the usual hour. He was a loyal and steadfast friend, who encouraged plainspoken disagreement with his opinions and delighted in being shown a better way. Finally, he was devout without being in the least superstitious. Remember all this so that in your final hour you too can depart this life with as clear a conscience as his.[40]

—Marcus Aurelius

'But the tyrant will chain – ' What will he chain? Your leg? 'He will chop off – ' What? Your head. What he will never chain or chop off is your integrity. That's the reason behind the ancient advice to 'know yourself.'[41]

—Epictetus

The essence of good and evil consists in the condition of our character. And externals are the means by which our character finds its particular good and evil. It finds its good by not attaching value to the means. Correct judgments about externals make our character good, as perverse or distorted ones make it bad.[42]

—Epictetus

Be as good as your word.[43]

—Seneca

Whenever externals are more important to you than your own integrity, then be prepared to serve them the remainder of your life. Don't hedge and agree to be their slave, then change your mind

later; commit to one or the other position at once and without
reserve. Choose to be either free or a slave, enlightened or a fool,
a thoroughbred or a nag. Either resign yourself to a life of abuse
till you die, or escape it immediately. For God's sake, don't put up
with years of abuse, and then change your mind! The humiliation
can be avoided before it begins: just decide now what you think
is truly good and bad.[44]

—Epictetus

I view with pleasure and approval the way you keep on at your
studies and sacrifice everything to your single-minded efforts
to make yourself every day a better man. I do not merely urge
you to persevere in this; I actually implore you to. Let me give
you, though, this one piece of advice: refrain from following the
example of those whose craving is for attention, not their own im-
provement, by doing certain things which are calculated to give
rise to comment on your appearance or way of living generally.[45]

—Seneca

For every challenge, remember the resources you have within you
to cope with it. Provoked by the sight of a handsome man or a
beautiful woman, you will discover within you the contrary power
of self-restraint. Faced with pain, you will discover the power of
endurance. If you are insulted, you will discover patience. In time,
you will grow to be confident that there is not a single impression
that you will not have the moral means to tolerate.[46]

—Epictetus

Whenever circumstance brings some welcome thing your way, stop
in suspicion and alarm: wild animals and fish alike are taken in by
this or that inviting prospect. Do you look on them as presents
given you by fortune? They are snares. Anyone among you who

wishes to lead a secure life will do his very best to steer well wide of these baited bounties, which comprise yet another instance of the errors we miserable creatures fall into: we think these things are ours when in fact it is we who are caught. That track leads to precipices; life on that giddy level ends in a fall. Once, moreover, prosperity begins to carry us off course, we are no more capable even of bringing the ship to a standstill than of going down with the consolation that she has been held on her course or of going down once and for all; fortune does not just capsize the boat: she hurls it headlong on the rocks and dashes it to pieces. Cling, therefore, to this sound and wholesome plan of life: indulge the body just so far as suffices for good health. It needs to be treated somewhat strictly to prevent it from being dishonest to the spirit. Your food should appease your hunger, your drink quench your thirst, your clothing keep out the cold, your house be a protection against inclement weather. It makes no difference whether it is built of turf or of variegated marble imported from another country: what you have to understand is that thatch makes a person just as good a roof as gold does. Spurn everything that is added on by way of decoration and display by unnecessary labor. Reflect that nothing merits admiration except the spirit, the impressiveness of which prevents it from being impressed by anything.[47]

—Seneca

> *If what troubles you arises from some flaw in your character... who prevents you from correcting the flaw?*
>
> - Marcus Aurelius

If you're troubled by something outside yourself, it isn't the thing itself that bothers you, but your opinion of it and this opinion you have the power to revoke immediately. If what troubles you arises from some flaw in your character or disposition, who prevents you from correcting the flaw? If it's your failure to do some good or necessary work that frustrates you, why not put your energy into doing it rather than fretting about it?[48]

—Marcus Aurelius

There is a world of difference between, on the one hand, choosing not to do what is wrong and, on the other, not knowing how to do it in the first place. They lacked the cardinal virtues of justice, moral insight, self-control, and courage. There were corresponding qualities, in each case not unlike these, that had a place in their primitive lives; but virtue only comes to a character which has been thoroughly schooled and trained and brought to a pitch of perfection by unremitting practice. We are born for it, but not with it. And even in the best of people, until you cultivate it there is only the material for virtue, not virtue itself.[49]

—Seneca

This much, however, seems to be an observed fact: that just as a powerfully built man, if deprived of sight, is apt to fall heavily when he moves about, because he cannot see, so too in the moral sphere; but if the subject acquires intelligence he becomes outstanding in conduct, and his disposition, instead of *resembling* virtue, will now *be* virtue in the full sense.[50]

—Aristotle

Socialize with men of good character, in order to model your life on theirs, whether you choose someone living or someone from the past.[51]

—Epictetus

We need to set our affections on some good man and keep him constantly before our eyes, so that we may live as if he were watching us and do everything as if he saw what we were doing... choose someone whose way of life as well as words, and whose very face as mirroring the character that lies behind it, have won your approval. Be always pointing him out to yourself either as your guardian or as your model. There is a need in my view, for someone as a standard against which our characters can measure themselves. Without a ruler to do it against you won't make the crooked straight.[52]

—Seneca

> *The truly good and wise man bears all his fortunes with dignity, and always takes the most honorable course.*
>
> - Aristotle

Yet the accidents of fortune are many, and they vary in importance. Little pieces of good luck (and likewise of the opposite kind) clearly do not disturb the tenor of our life. On the other hand many great strokes of fortune, if favorable, will make life more felicitous (since they tend naturally of themselves to add to its attractions, and also they can be used in a fine and responsible way); but if they fall out adversely they restrict and spoil our felicity, both by inflicting pain and by putting a check on many of our activities. Nevertheless even here, when a man bears patiently a number of heavy disasters, not because he does not feel them but because he has a high and generous nature, his nobility shines through. And if, as we said, the quality of a life is determined by its activities, no man who is truly happy can become miserable; because he will never do things that are hateful and mean. For we believe that the truly good and wise man bears all his fortunes with dignity, and always takes the most honorable course that circumstances permit...[53]

—Aristotle

I shall put myself under observation straight away and undertake a review of my day – a course which is of the utmost benefit. What really ruins our characters is the fact that none of us looks back over his life. We think about what we are going to do, and only rarely of that, and fail to think about what we have done, yet any plans for the future are dependent on the past.[54]

—Seneca

Some thinkers hold that it is by nature that people become good, others that it is by habit and others that it is by instruction. The bounty of nature is clearly beyond our control; it is bestowed by some divine dispensation upon those who are truly fortunate. It is a regrettable fact that discussion and instruction are not effective in all cases; just as the piece of land has to be prepared beforehand if it is to nourish the seed, so the mind of the pupil has to be prepared in its habits if it is to enjoy and dislike the right things; because the man who lives in accordance with his feelings would not listen to an argument to dissuade him, or understand it if he did. And when a man is in that state, how is it possible to persuade him out of it? In general, feeling seems to yield not to argument but only to force. Therefore we must have a character to work on that has some affinity to virtue: one that appreciates what is noble and objects to what is base.[55]

—Aristotle

Do not get rich by evil actions, and let not any one ever be able to reproach you with speaking against those who partake of your friendship.[56]

—Thales

In order to be a good man one must first have been brought up in the right way and trained in the right habits, and must thereafter spend one's life in reputable occupations, doing no wrong either with or against one's will: then this can be achieved by living under the guidance of some intelligence or right system that has effective force.[57]

—Aristotle

> *Success tends to create pride and blindness in the hearts of men, while suffering teaches them to be patient and strong.*
>
> - Xenophon

In my experience, men who respond to good fortune with modesty and kindness are harder to find than those who face adversity with courage. For in the very nature of things, success tends to create pride and blindness in the hearts of men, while suffering teaches them to be patient and strong.[58]

—Xenophon

For I believe that the best life is lived by those who take the best care to make themselves as good as possible, and the pleasantest life by those who are most conscious that they are becoming better.[59]

—Socrates

It is more revealing to see a man in doubt and peril, to learn who he may be in hostile situations, for only then are truthful words squeezed out from the bottom of his heart – his façade is torn away, what he truly is remains.[60]

—Lucretius

The citizen who contributes nothing of value to the community receives no honor; for it is the benefactor of the community that receives what it has to give, namely honor.[61]

—Aristotle

> *The citizen who contributes nothing of value to the community receives no honor.*
>
> - Aristotle

Make sure you're not made 'Emperor,' avoid that imperial stain. It can happen to you so keep yourself simple, good, pure, saintly, plain, a friend to justice, god-fearing, gracious, affectionate, and

strong for your proper work. Fight to remain the person that philosophy wished to make you. Revere the gods, and look after each other. Life is short – the fruit of this life is a good character and acts for the common good.[62]
—Marcus Aurelius

Would you have a great empire? Rule over yourself![63]
—Publilius Syrus

Impulse [desire] shall obey reason; for there is no better way than this to secure the observance of duties.[64]
—Cicero

But what does Socrates say? 'One person likes tending to his farm, another to his horse; I like to daily monitor my self-improvement.'[65]
—Socrates as quoted by Epictetus

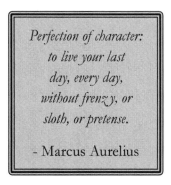

*Perfection of character: to live your last day, every day, without frenzy, or sloth, or pretense.*

- Marcus Aurelius

Perfection of character: to live your last day, every day, without frenzy, or sloth, or pretense.[66]
—Marcus Aurelius

These men – worthy of their city. We who remain behind may hope to be spared their fate, but must resolve to keep the same daring spirit against the foe. It is not simply a question of estimating the advantages in theory. I could tell you a long story about what is to be gained by beating the enemy back. What I would prefer is that you should fix your eyes every day on the greatness of Athens as she really is, and should fall in love with her. When you realize her greatness, then reflect that what made her great was men with a spirit of adventure, men who knew their duty, men who were ashamed to fall below a certain standard. If they ever failed in an enterprise, they made up their minds that at any rate the city should not find their courage lacking to her, and they gave her their lives, to her and all of us.[67]

—Pericles

All I do is to go about and try to persuade you, both young and old, not to care for your bodies or your monies first, and to care more exceedingly for the soul, to make it as good as possible; and I tell you that virtue comes not from money, but from virtue comes both money and all other good things for mankind, both in private and in public.[68]

—Socrates

Then what makes a beautiful human being? Isn't it the presence of human excellence? Young friend, if you wish to be beautiful, then work diligently at human excellence. And what is that? Observe those whom you praise without prejudice. The just or the unjust? The just. The even-tempered or the undisciplined? The even-tempered. The self-controlled or the uncontrolled? The self-controlled. In making yourself that kind of person, you will become beautiful – but to the extent you ignore these qualities, you'll be ugly, even if you use every trick in the book to appear beautiful.[69]

—Epictetus

This is what you should teach me, how to be like Odysseus – how to love my country, wife and father, and how, even after suffering shipwreck, I might keep sailing on course to those honorable ends.[70]

—Seneca

> *Very little is needed for everything to be upset and ruined, only a slight lapse in reason.*
>
> - Epictetus

Bear this in mind and you will everywhere preserve your proper character; forget it and I assure you that your time here will be a waste, and whatever care you are now expending on yourself will all go down the drain. Very little is needed for everything to be upset and ruined, only a slight lapse in reason. It's much easier for a mariner to wreck his ship than it is for him to keep it sailing safely; all he has to do is head a little more upwind and disaster is instantaneous. In fact, he does not have to do anything: a momentary loss of attention will produce the same result.[71]

—Epictetus

It is right for the good man to be self-loving, because then he will both be benefited himself by performing fine actions and also help others...But it is also true to say of the man of good character that he performs many actions for the sake of his friends and his country, and if necessary even dies for them. For he will sacrifice both money and honors and in general the goods that people struggle to obtain in his pursuit of what is morally fine.[72]

—Aristotle

We all look with distaste on people who arrogantly pretend to a reputation to which they are not entitled; but equally to be condemned are those who, through lack of moral fiber, fail to live up to the reputation which is theirs already.[73]
—Thucydides

Where you arrive does not matter so much as what sort of person you are when you arrive there.[74]
—Seneca

Never shirk the proper dispatch of your duty, no matter if you are freezing or hot, groggy or well-rested, vilified or praised, not even if dying or pressed by other demands. Even dying is one of the important assignments of life and, in this as in all else, make the most of your resources to do well the duty at hand.[75]
—Marcus Aurelius

Leaders must always set the highest standard. In a summer campaign, leaders must always endure their share of the sun and the heat and, in winter, the cold and the frost. In all labors, leaders must prove tireless if they want to enjoy the trust of their followers.[76]
—Xenophon

Even in death, a good man would not deceive.[77]
—Publius Syrus

Don't behave as if you are destined to live forever. What's fated hangs over you. As long as you live and while you can, become good now.[78]
—Marcus Aurelius

> *Good people will
> do what they find
> honorable to do, even if
> it requires hard work;
> they'll do it even if it
> causes them injury;
> they'll do it even if it
> will bring danger.*
>
> - Seneca

Good people will do what they find honorable to do, even if it requires hard work; they'll do it even if it causes them injury; they'll do it even if it will bring danger. Again, they won't do what they find base, even if it brings wealth, pleasure, or power. Nothing will deter them from what is honorable, and nothing will lure them into what is base.[79]

—Seneca

Do the right thing. The rest doesn't matter.[80]

—Marcus Aurelius

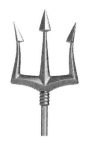

BOOK 2

# COURAGE

We often see examples of heroic men and women displaying acts of courage in movies and on the news that are simply awe-inspiring; the brave Marine who jumps on a grenade to shield others, the firefighter who rushes into a burning building to rescue a family, or the teacher who confronts a gunman to stop a school shooting. As a result of seeing these visceral images, people often think of courage solely in the physical sense, and this is an important aspect. After all, as Pericles tells us, we need to be able to "stand up to danger."

However, courage comes in several forms, and as leaders, it is often just as important to not only show physical courage, but moral courage as well. Exercising moral courage can be incredibly difficult, whether it means holding your team accountable, confronting a peer, or standing up to your boss. If you're ever challenged in a situation where you need to decide how to act with moral courage, think of two main questions: 1) Is it the right thing to do? and 2) Does it benefit the team? If the answer to both of these questions is yes, then you'll know the situation requires you to act.

Courage is the first of human qualities because it is the quality which guarantees the others.[81]
　　—Aristotle

Fortune favors the brave.[82]
　　—Latin Proverb, attributed to Pliny the Elder

We set our stakes...in our people's courage to act.[83]
　　—Pericles

Let us begin with courage...it is a mean state in relation to feelings of fear and confidence.[84]
　　—Aristotle

Freedom cannot be won without sacrifice.[85]
　　—Seneca

Now always be the best, my boy, the bravest, and hold your head up high above the others.[86]
　　—Homer

I prefer the man who stands up to danger rather than the one who runs away from it.[87]
　　—Pericles

Our salvation, therefore, is in the might of our hands and in hard fighting.[88]
　　—Homer

Perhaps someone may say: Are you not ashamed then, Socrates, at having followed such a practice that now you run a risk of a sentence of death? I would answer such a one fairly: You are wrong, my friend, if you think a man with a spark of decency in him ought to calculate life or death; the only thing he ought to consider, if he does anything, is whether he does right or wrong, whether it is what a good man does or a bad man...Wherever a man takes his stand, whether in accord with his own best judgment or in obedience to his commander's orders, that's where he needs to plant his feet and face every danger, careless of death and of everything but dishonor.[89]

—Socrates

> *Wherever a man takes his stand... that's where he needs to plant his feet and face every danger, careless of death and of everything but dishonor.*
>
> - Socrates

The man who shuns and fears everything and stands up to nothing becomes a coward; the man who is afraid of nothing at all, but marches up to every danger, becomes foolhardy. Similarly, the man who indulges in every pleasure and refrains from none becomes licentious; but if a man behaves like a boor and turns his back on every pleasure, he is a case of insensibility. Thus, temperance and courage are destroyed by excess and deficiency and preserved by the mean.[90]

—Aristotle

> *The man who shuns*
> *and fears everything*
> *and stands up to*
> *nothing is a coward;*
> *the man who is*
> *afraid of nothing*
> *at all, but marches*
> *up to every danger,*
> *becomes foolhardy.*
>
> - Aristotle

The spot where a person decides to station himself, or wherever his commanding officer stations him – well, I think that's where he ought to take his stand and face the enemy, and not worry about being killed, or about anything but doing his duty.[91]

—Marcus Aurelius

I will be choosing to die rather than to remain alive without freedom and beg, as an alternative to death, a vastly inferior life.[92]

—Xenophon

Courage cannot be cast down by adversity.[93]

—Publius Syrus

I am not afraid of an army of lions led by a sheep; I am afraid of an army of sheep led by a lion.[94]

—Alexander the Great

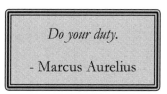

*Do your duty.*

- Marcus Aurelius

Do your duty—and never mind whether you are shivering or warm, sleeping on your feet or in your bed, hearing yourself slandered or praised, dying or doing something else. Yes, even dying is an act of life and should be done, like everything else, "to the best of your abilities."[95]

—Marcus Aurelius

In the face of danger, be eager, not intimidated.[96]

—Xenophon

It is not reasonable that he who does not shoot should hit the mark, nor that he who does not stand fast at his post should win the day, or that the helpless man should succeed or the coward prosper.[97]

—Plutarch

A man of courage never endures an insult; an honorable man never offers one.[98]

—Publius Syrus

When any man is foremost in defending his fellows from danger, and braves and awaits the onslaught of the most powerful beasts, it is natural that he should receive marks of favor and honor from the people, while the man who acts in the opposite manner will meet with reprobation and dislike.[99]

—Polybius

I should prefer to be free from torture, but if the time comes when it must be endured, I shall desire that I may conduct myself therein with bravery, honor, and courage. Of course I prefer that war should not occur; but if war does occur, I shall desire that I may nobly endure the wounds, the starvation, and all that the exigency of war brings. Nor am I so mad as to crave illness; but if I must suffer illness, I shall desire that I may do nothing which shows lack of restraint, and nothing that is unmanly. The conclusion is, not that hardships are desirable, but that virtue is desirable, which enables us patiently to endure hardships.[100]

 —Seneca

It is the mark of a courageous man to face things that are terrible to a human being, and that he can see are such, because it is a fine act to face them and a disgrace not to do so. This is why it is thought to be a better proof of courage to remain calm and undismayed in sudden alarms than in those that are foreseen: the action proceeds more directly from the moral state, because it is less the result of preparation. One may choose to face a foreseeable danger after calculation and reflection, but one faces sudden dangers only in virtue of the formed state of character.[101]

 —Aristotle

An honorable death is better than a disgraceful life.[102]

 —Publius Syrus

When she created us, nature endowed us with noble aspirations, and just as she gave certain animals ferocity, others timidity, others cunning, so to us she gave a spirit of exalted ambition, a spirit that takes us in search of life of, not the greatest safety, but the greatest honor – a spirit very like the universe, which, so far as mortal footsteps may, it follows and adopts as a model. It is

self-assertive; it feels assured of honor and respect; it is a master
of all things; it is above all things; it should accordingly give in
to nothing; in nothing should it see a burden calculated to bow
the shoulders of a man.[103]

—Seneca

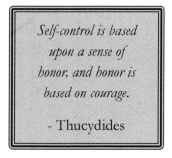

*Self-control is based upon a sense of honor, and honor is based on courage.*

- Thucydides

We are both brave in war and wise in council. Brave, because
self-control is based upon a sense of honor, and honor is based
on courage. And we are wise because we are not so highly educated as to look down upon our laws and customs, and are too
rigorously trained in self-control to be able to disobey them.[104]

—Thucydides

What is terrible is not the same for all persons. There is a kind
of thing that we describe as beyond human endurance, and this
is fearful to any reasonable person; but things within the limits
of human endurance differ in the magnitude and intensity of
the fear that they inspire (and similarly with things that inspire
confidence). The courageous man, however, is undaunted, so far
as is humanly possible; he will fear what it is natural for man to
fear, but he will face it in the right way and as principle directs,
for the sake of what is right and honorable, for this is the end
of virtue. But it is possible to fear these things too much or too
little, and also to fear what is not fearful as if it were. One kind

of error is to be afraid of the wrong thing, another to be afraid in the wrong way, and another at the wrong time or with some other such qualification (and similarly with things that inspire confidence). The man who faces and fears (or similarly feels confident about) the right things for the right reason and in the right way and at the right time is courageous (for the courageous man feels and acts duly, and as principle directs); and the end of every activity is that which accords with the disposition corresponding to that activity. This is true of the courageous man. His courage is a noble thing, so its end is of the same kind, because the nature of any given thing is determined by its end. Thus it is for a right and noble motive that the courageous man faces the dangers and performs the actions appropriate to his courage.[105]

—Aristotle

Famous men have the whole earth as their memorial: it is not only the inscriptions on their graves in their own country that mark them out; no, in foreign lands also, not in any visible form but in people's hearts, their memory abides and grows. It is for you to try to be like them. Make up your minds that happiness depends on being free, and freedom depends on being courageous. Let there be no relaxation in face of the perils of war.[106]

—Pericles

I would rather die having spoken in my manner, than speak in your manner and live. For neither in war nor yet in law ought any man use every way of escaping death. For often in battle there is no doubt that if a man will throw away his arms, and fall on his knees before his pursuers, he may escape death, if a man is willing to say or do anything. The difficulty, my friends, is not in avoiding death, but in avoiding unrighteousness; for that runs deeper than death.[107]

—Socrates

A glorious death is his
who for his country falls.[108]
—Homer

How does it help, my husband, to make misfortune heavier
by complaining about it? This is more fit for a king – to seize
your adversities head on. The more precarious his situation, the
more imminent his fall from power, the more firmly he should
be resolved to stand and fight. It isn't manly to retreat from
misfortune.[109]
—Seneca

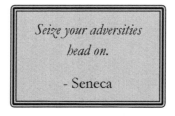

*Seize your adversities
head on.*

- Seneca

Not courage alone, therefore, but an actual sense of your superiority should animate you as you go forward against the
enemy. Confidence, out of a mixture of ignorance and good
luck, can be felt even by cowards; but this sense of superiority
comes only to those who, like us, have real reasons for knowing
that they are better placed than their opponents. And when the
chances on both sides are equal, it is intelligence that confirms
courage – the intelligence that makes one able to look down
on one's opponent, and which proceeds not by hoping for the
best (a method only valuable in desperate situations), but by estimating what the facts are, and thus obtaining a clearer vision
of what to expect.[110]
—Thucydides

Do not act unwillingly, or selfishly, or impulsively, or tentatively. Do not dress your thought in much fine talk. Be short in speech and restrained in action. Let the god who dwells within you command a manly man, a seasoned veteran, a statesman, a Roman, a leader who stands ready to give up his life when the retreat is sounded, without requiring an oath or looking around for witnesses. Show by a cheerful look that you don't need the help or comfort of others. Standing up – not propped up.[111]

—Marcus Aurelius

A man who follows someone else not only does not find anything, he is not even looking. 'But surely you are going to walk in your predecessors' footsteps?' Yes indeed, I shall use the old road, but if I find a shorter and easier one I shall open it up. The men who pioneered the old routes are leaders, not our masters. Truth lies open to everyone. There has yet to be a monopoly of truth. And there is plenty of it left for future generations too.[112]

—Seneca

I think that just as one body is born with more strength than another for doing work, so one mind is naturally endowed with greater fortitude than another for facing danger; for I observe that people who are brought up under the same laws and customs differ greatly in courage. But I think that every natural disposition can be developed in the direction of fortitude by instruction and application...everyone, whether his natural ability is above or below the average, ought to study and exercise any qualities for which he wishes to earn recognition.[113]

—Socrates

Real courage never alters, and those who have it never use inexperience as an excuse for being anything else but courageous. So far as you are concerned you may lack the enemy's experience, but that is more than made up for by your superior daring. This skill of theirs, which is the thing which you fear most, has to be combined with courage. Then, in the hour of danger, they will remember how to do what they have learnt to do. But if a stout heart is lacking, all the skill in the world will not avail in the face of peril. Fear drives out all memory of previous instruction, and without the will to resist, skill is useless.[114]

—Thucydides

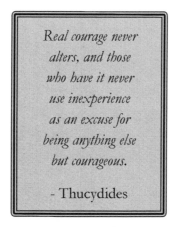

*Real courage never alters, and those who have it never use inexperience as an excuse for being anything else but courageous.*

- Thucydides

What we can do is adopt a noble spirit, such a spirit as befits a good man, so that we may bear up bravely under all that fortune sends us and bring our wills in tune with nature's; reversals, after all, are the means by which nature regulates this visible realm of hers.[115]

—Seneca

I count it as highly indicative of good leadership when people obey someone without coercion and are prepared to remain by him during times of danger.[116]

—Socrates

We must realize, too, that, both for cities and for individuals, it is from the greatest dangers that the greatest glory is to be won.[117]
—Thucydides

With courage; it is by habituating ourselves to make light of alarming situations and to face them that we become brave, and it is when we have become brave that we shall be most able to face an alarming situation.[118]
—Aristotle

The disgrace incurred by cowardice is far more painful than death.[119]
—Pericles

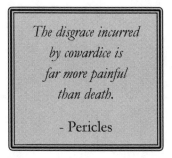

*The disgrace incurred by cowardice is far more painful than death.*

- Pericles

Death and pain are not frightening, it's the fear of pain and death we need to fear. Which is why we praise the poet who wrote 'Death is not fearful, but dying like a coward is.'[120]
—Epictetus

Don't fear the future. You will face it, if that is your fate, armed with the same reason that protects and guides you in the present.[121]
—Marcus Aurelius

Don't fear death, but give it a friendly greeting. Nature sends it along with everything else. Like youth and old age, growing up and reaching one's prime, growing teeth and a beard and white hair, begetting and conceiving and bearing children—our own dissolution is just one of life's natural processes. A man who has given it any thought will never approach death carelessly, hastily, or scornfully, but he will wait for it as he would for any natural process.[122]

—Marcus Aurelius

Glorious are the deeds of those who undergo labor and run the risk of danger.[123]

—Alexander the Great

The bravest are surely those who have the clearest vision of what is before them, glory and danger alike, and yet notwithstanding, go out to meet it.[124]

—Thucydides

Whatever your mission, stick by it as if it were a law and you would be committing sacrilege to betray it. Pay no attention whatever people might say; this no longer should influence you.[125]

—Epictetus

> *Whatever your mission, stick by it as if it were a law and you would be committing sacrilege to betray it.*
>
> - Epictetus

BOOK 3
# COMPASSION

As a leader (and as a good human), it is imperative to be in sync with your compassionate side. If you do not understand compassion, then you cannot possibly understand the daily trials, tribulations, and suffering of your people. If you cannot understand and relate to it, then how could you ever hope to improve the situation?

Compassion builds your emotional intelligence – or the ability to not only effectively control your emotions but to understand the emotions of others – an essential component of effective leadership. Through this lens you can better understand where your people are coming from, what motivates and drives them, and you will ultimately be better equipped to lead them.

Live in harmony with everyone around you, and love—without reservations or conditions—those with whom you live and work.[126]

—Marcus Aurelius

It is within a man's power to love even those who sin against him. This becomes possible when you realize that they are your brothers, that they wrong you unintentionally or out of ignorance, that in a little while you and they will be dead, and above all, that they have not really hurt you so long as you have not sullied your conscience or damaged your inner self by responding in kind.[127]

—Marcus Aurelius

> *It is within a man's power to love even those who sin against him.*
>
> - Marcus Aurelius

Herodotus tells us that the Medes always chose a good man to be their king, because they wanted to make sure they would receive just treatment. And our own ancestors, I believe, felt the same. For when the Roman populace began to be oppressed by certain dominant individuals, they themselves chose another citizen, a man of outstanding character, to be their monarch and their protector. His job was to defend the weaker members of the community against tyranny and to establish equitable conditions which guaranteed equal rights to the grand and humble alike.[128]

—Cicero

Nature bids us to do well by all...Wherever there is a human being, we have an opportunity for kindness.[129]

—Seneca

*Wherever there is a human being, we have an opportunity for kindness.*

- Seneca

When you have trouble getting out of bed in the morning, remember that your defining characteristic – what defines a human being – is to work with others.[130]

—Marcus Aurelius

If those who stand in your way cannot turn you from the path of reason and stop you from doing what is right, why should they be able to prevent you from treating them kindly? Stand guard in both respects: be tough-minded in thought and action while being gentle to those who oppose or annoy you. It is as much a weakness to become harsh as it is to shrink from action and relent out of fear. Both alike abandon their posts: the one who panics, the other who is estranged form a natural brother and friend.[131]

—Marcus Aurelius

It is the mark of a good friend to help those who are in need.[132]

—Aristotle

First thing every morning tell yourself: today I am going to meet a busybody, an ingrate, a bully, a liar, a schemer, and a boor.

Ignorance of good and evil has made them what they are. But I know that the good is by nature beautiful and the bad ugly, and I know that these wrong-doers are by nature my brothers, not by blood or breeding, but by being similarly endowed with reason and sharing in the divine. None of them can harm me, for none can force me to do wrong against my will, and I cannot be angry with a brother or resent him, for we were born into this world to work together like the feet, the hands, eyelids, and upper and lower rows of teeth. To work against one another is contrary to nature, and what could be more like working against someone than resenting or abandoning him?[133]

—Marcus Aurelius

> *None of them can harm me, for none can force me to do wrong against my will.*
>
> - Marcus Aurelius

Philosophers say that people are all guided by a single standard. When they assent to a thing it is because they feel it must be true, when they dissent, it is because they feel something isn't true, and when they suspend judgment, it is because they feel that the thing is unclear. Similarly, they say that in the case of impulse people feel that its object must be to their advantage, and that it is impossible to consider any one thing advantageous and desire something different, or consider one thing right and have an impulse to do something else.

If all this is true, then what grounds do we have for being angry with anyone? We use labels like 'thief' and 'robber' in connection with them, but what do these words mean? They merely signify that people are confused about what is good and what is bad. So should we be angry with them, or should we pity them instead? Show them where they go wrong and you will find that they'll reform. But unless they see it, they are stuck with nothing better than their usual opinion as their practical guide.[134]
    —Epictetus

"No one," said Plato, "knowingly chooses to live without the truth." Or without justice, wisdom, compassion, and the like. Keep this thought perpetually in mind, and you will treat everyone more gently.[135]
    —Marcus Aurelius

He who lives only for himself is truly dead to others.[136]
    —Publius Syrus

Let this be your one joy and delight: to go from one act of kindness to another with your mind fixed on God.[137]
    —Marcus Aurelius

You will find that an act of kindness done at the right moment has a power to dispel old grievances quite out of proportion to the act itself.[138]
    —Thucydides

Learn to concentrate on what those around you are saying. Enter as deeply as possible into the mind of each speaker.[139]
    —Marcus Aurelius

There is a deep—and usually frustrated—desire in the heart of everyone to act with benevolence rather than selfishness, and one fine instance of generosity can inspire dozens more.[140]
—Xenophon

> *One fine instance*
> *of generosity can*
> *inspire dozens more.*
>
> *- Xenophon*

When you start to lose your temper, remember: There's nothing manly about rage. It's courtesy and kindness that define a human being. That's who possesses strength and nerves and guts, not the angry whiners. To react like that brings you closer to impassivity – and so to strength.[141]
—Marcus Aurelius

The man who gets angry at the right things and with the right people, and also in the right way and at the right time and for the right length of time, is commended; so this person will be patient, inasmuch as patience is commendable, because a patient person tends to be unperturbed and not carried away by his feelings, but indignant only in the way and on the grounds and for the length of time that his principle prescribes. He is considered to err, if at all, on the side of deficiency, because the patient man is not revengeful; he is more inclined to be forgiving.[142]
—Aristotle

When your spirits need a lift, think of the virtues and talents of those around you—one's energy, another's modesty, the generosity of a third, something else in a fourth. Nothing is so inspiring or uplifting as the sight of these splendid qualities in our friends. Keep them always in mind.[143]

—Marcus Aurelius

Whenever you meet someone, ask yourself straightaway: What are the things that this person deems good and evil? For if he holds certain beliefs about pleasure and pain and the causes of each, about fame and obscurity, or about death and life, then I won't think it surprising or weird if he behaves in a certain way. Indeed, I'll regard it as inevitable.[144]

—Marcus Aurelius

A spirit of freedom governs our conduct; not only in public affairs, but also in managing the small tensions of everyday life, where we show no animosity at our neighbor's choice of pleasures, nor cast aspersions that may hurt even if they do not harm.[145]

—Pericles

If someone makes a mistake, correct him with kindness and point out where he went wrong. If you fail, blame only yourself, or better yet, don't blame anyone.[146]

—Marcus Aurelius

Hecato says, 'I can teach you a love potion made without any drugs, herbs, or special spell – if you would be loved, love.'[147]

—Seneca

Love your fellow man.[148]

—Marcus Aurelius

We are not born for ourselves alone, but our country claims a share of our being, and our friends a share.[149]

—Cicero

*We are not born for ourselves alone.*

- Cicero

Someone despises me.
That's their problem.
Mine: not to do or say anything despicable.
Someone hates me. Their problem.
Mine: to be patient and cheerful with everyone, including them. Ready to show them their mistake. Not spitefully, or to show off my own self-control, but in an honest, upright way...That's what we should be like inside, and never let the gods catch us feeling anger or resentment. As long as you do what's proper to your nature, and accept what the world's nature has in store – as long as you work for others' good, by any and all means – what is there that can harm you?[150]

—Marcus Aurelius

Kindness is invincible, provided it's sincere – not ironic or an act. What can even the most vicious person do if you keep treating him with kindness and gently set him straight – if you get the chance – correcting him cheerfully at the exact moment that he's trying to do you harm.[151]

—Marcus Aurelius

It is in accordance with Nature to show affection for our friends, and to rejoice in their advancement as if it were absolutely our own. For if we have not done this, even virtue, which grows strong only through exercising our perceptions, will not abide with us.[152]
  —Seneca

The good man feels towards his friend as he feels towards himself, because his friend is a second self to him.[153]
  —Aristotle

The man who fails to understand what goes on in the world is as much a stranger to the world as he who is ignorant of how the world is made. He is a fugitive running from the law; a blind man whose eyes cannot see reason, a beggar leaning on others and incapable of standing on his own feet; a pustule on the face of the earth because he has separated himself from the reasonable law that holds the world together by declaring his displeasure with this or that (and forgetting that he too is a "this or that"): an amputated body part, severed from the fellowship of all rational souls, one and indivisible.[154]
  —Marcus Aurelius

I am convinced that people are much better off when their whole city is flourishing than when certain citizens prosper but the community itself has gone off course. When a man is doing well for himself but his country is falling to pieces he goes to pieces along with it, but a struggling individual has much better hopes if his country is thriving. A city can bear its people's various sufferings but no single person can bear the whole city's, so you should all be working together to end them and quit what you are doing now: wallowing in your personal miseries at the expense of collective recovery.[155]
  —Pericles

As you move forward along the path of reason, people will stand in your way. They will never be able to keep you from doing what's sound, so don't let them knock out your goodwill for them. Keep a steady watch on both fronts, not only for well-based judgments and actions, but also for gentleness with those who would obstruct our path or create other difficulties. For getting angry is also a weakness, just as abandoning the task or surrendering under panic. For doing either is an equal desertion – the one by shrinking back and the other by estrangement from family and friend.[156]

—Marcus Aurelius

> *Getting angry is also a weakness, just as abandoning the task or surrendering under panic.*
>
> - Marcus Aurelius

Which one of you does not admire what Lycurgus the Spartan said? He was blinded in one eye by a young citizen of Sparta, who was then handed over to Lycurgus to punish as he saw fit. Lycurgus not only declined to exact revenge, he gave the youth an education and made a good man of him. He then publicly introduced him at the theatre. The Spartans were indignant, but Lycurgus said, 'The person you gave me was violent and aggressive; I'm returning him to you civilized and refined.'[157]

—Epictetus

When someone wrongs you, ask yourself: What made him do it? Once you understand his concept of good and evil, you'll feel sorry for him and cease to be either amazed or angry. If his concept is similar to yours, then you are bound to forgive him since you would have acted as he did in similar circumstances. But if you do not share his ideas of good and evil, then you should find it even easier to overlook the wrongs of someone who is confused and in a moral muddle.[158]

—Marcus Aurelius

Whenever anyone criticizes or wrongs you, remember that they are only doing or saying what they think is right. They cannot be guided by your views, only their own; so if their views are wrong, they are the ones who suffer insofar as they are misguided...With this in mind you will treat your critic with more compassion. Say to yourself each time, 'He did what he believed was right.'[159]

—Epictetus

Joy for human beings lies in proper human work. And proper human work consists in: acts of kindness to other human beings, disdain for the stirrings of the senses, identifying trustworthy impressions, and contemplating the natural order and all that happens in keeping with it.[160]

—Marcus Aurelius

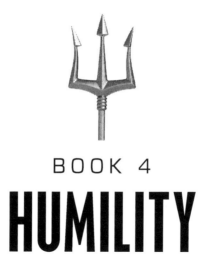

## BOOK 4

# HUMILITY

Humility is perhaps the most underrated leadership trait, yet one of the most vital. Having a deep, guiding sense of humility means listening first before acting; it means recognizing that you do not have all of the answers; and it means that sometimes the best idea can come from the most junior person.

Unfortunately, most of us have seen individuals who do not embody the humility necessary for leadership. If you haven't seen this firsthand, here's what leaders who lack humility look like: they dismiss valid ideas raised by members of their team; they believe that employees who are smarter than they are threatens their leadership; they make excuses and hide mistakes; they consistently put their own interests above the group, and as a result, they fail to get the best out of their teams.

On the other side of the spectrum, the best humble leaders are those who are able to capitalize on the collective knowledge, experience, talent, and abilities of their team. They admit when they make mistakes. They do not care who gets the credit. They take responsibility and ownership. And time and time again, they are willing to always put the team's goals ahead of their own.

The beginnings of all things are small.[161]
—Cicero

Self-confidence should always ride side by side with a strong sense of humility.[162]
—Xenophon

Modest in victory; graceful in defeat.[163]
—Marcus Aurelius

Treat your inferiors as you would treat your betters.[164]
—Seneca

Do not find your happiness in another's sorrow.[165]
—Publius Syrus

Pride is a byproduct of blissful ignorance and a quality inherent to cowards.[166]
—Pericles

Zeno would also say that nothing is more hostile to a firm grasp of knowledge than self-deception.[167]
—Diogenes Laertius

The founder of the universe, who assigned to us the laws of life, provided that we should live well, but not in luxury. Everything needed for our well-being is right before us, whereas what luxury requires is gathered by many miseries and anxieties. Let us use this gift of nature and count it among the greatest things.[168]
—Seneca

No person has the power to have everything they want, but it is in their power not to want what they don't have, and to cheerfully put to good use what they do have.[169]

—Seneca

That which isn't good for the hive, isn't good for the bee.[170]

—Marcus Aurelius

> *That which isn't good*
> *for the hive, isn't*
> *good for the bee.*
>
> - Marcus Aurelius

Take refuge in philosophy...Let her strip off your faults, rather than assist you to decry the faults of others.[171]

—Seneca

Drop this readiness to take offense. Who are you to use those common curses, like 'These damned fools,' etc.? Let them be. Since when are you so intelligent as to go around correcting other people's mistakes?[172]

—Epictetus

I am one of those who are very willing to be refuted if I say anything which is not true, and very willing to refute anyone else who says what is not true, and quite as ready to be refuted as to refute; for I hold that this is the greater gain of the two, just as the gain is greater of being cured of a very great evil than of curing another. For I imagine that there is no evil which a man can endure so great as an erroneous opinion about the matters of which we are speaking; and if you claim to be one of my sort, let us have the discussion out, but if you would rather have done, no matter; let us make an end of it.[173]

—Socrates

Surrounded as we are by such people – so confused, so ignorant of what they're saying and whatever faults they may or may not have, where those faults came from and how to get rid of them – I think we too should make a habit of asking ourselves, 'Could it be that I'm one of them too? What illusion about myself do I entertain? How do I regard myself – as another wise man, as someone with perfect self-control? Do I, too, ever make that boast about being prepared for whatever may happen? If I don't know something, am I properly aware that I don't know it?'[174]

—Epictetus

Whenever you are about to find fault with someone, ask yourself the following question: What fault of mine most nearly resembles the one I am about to criticize? Is it love of money? Or pleasure? Or reputation? And so on until you have identified the closest cousin. By redirecting your attention in this way, you will soon forget your anger as you realize that he can't help himself any more than you can. How can he possibly overcome the compulsion to do wrong? If you can help him with this, you have helped yourself as well.[175]

—Marcus Aurelius

A man whose ears are so completely closed to the truth that he cannot even hear it from a friend is a hopeless case. Cato spoke shrewdly, as so often, when he remarked, 'In some ways our worst enemies do us greater services than our friends who seem so agreeable: since enemies often tell us the truth, whereas friends never do.'[176]

—Cicero

As Plato said, every soul is deprived of truth against its will. The same holds true for justice, self-control, goodwill to others, and every similar virtue. It's essential to constantly keep this in your mind, for it will make you more gentle to all.[177]

—Marcus Aurelius

Humanity is the quality which stops one being arrogant towards one's fellows, or being acrimonious. In words, in actions, in emotions she reveals herself as kind and good-natured towards all. To her the troubles of anyone else are her own, and anything that benefits herself she welcomes primarily because it will be of benefit to someone else.[178]

—Seneca

Someone was preferred above you at a formal dinner or awards banquet, and their advice was solicited before yours. If such marks of esteem are good, you should be pleased for the other person; if they are not, don't chafe because you did not get them. And remember if you do not engage in the same acts as others with a view to gaining such honors, you cannot expect the same results.[179]

—Epictetus

What angers me are all those kings who are fabled for the heaps of gold in their coffers, and their freedom from trouble and pain. I have a different vision. I say that the true leader shuns luxury and ease. Once in power, he should want to work harder than ever.[180]

—Xenophon

> *The true leader shuns*
> *luxury and ease.*
> *Once in power, he*
> *should want to work*
> *harder than ever.*
>
> - Xenophon

Cherish your gifts, however humble, and take pleasure in them. Spend the rest of your days looking only to the gods from whom comes every good gift...[181]

—Marcus Aurelius

Consider, on the other hand, history's examples of success, and promotion to high civil and military office, and victory in the field. These, too, contain an element of chance. Nevertheless, whether for good or ill, no man on earth could ever have achieved them without the cooperation and resources contributed by other human beings.[182]

—Cicero

What an infinitesimal fraction of time's fathomless abyss is assigned to each of us! An instant, and it flickers out in eternity. What a speck in the plenitude of being we are! What a crumb in the bounty of life! How tiny on this broad earth the clod we crawl upon! Be mindful of all this, think nothing important except to do what your nature directs and to endure what the universal nature sends.[183]

—Marcus Aurelius

When you see someone often flashing their rank or position, or someone whose name is often bandied about in public, don't be envious; such things are bought at the expense of life...Some die on the first rungs of the ladder of success, others before they can reach the top, and the few that make it to the top of their ambition through a thousand indignities realize at the end it's only for an inscription on their gravestone.[184]

—Seneca

"My student days are over!" Nevertheless, you can still learn to check your arrogance, learn to rise above pleasure and pain, learn to ignore flattery, and learn not only to keep from being upset with the gauche and ungrateful, but to give them a helping hand![185]

—Marcus Aurelius

No one can be a friend unless he is a good man. But next to goodness itself, I entreat you to regard friendship as the finest thing in all the world.[186]

—Cicero

Above all, it is necessary for a man to estimate himself truly, because we commonly think that we can do more than we are able.[187]

—Seneca

If anyone can refute me – show me I'm making a mistake or looking at things from the wrong perspective – I'll gladly change. It's the truth I'm after, and the truth never harmed anyone. What harms us is to persist in self-deceit and ignorance.[188]

—Marcus Aurelius

> *If anyone can refute me — show me I'm making a mistake or looking at things from the wrong perspective — I'll gladly change.*
>
> - Marcus Aurelius

Get rid of your presuppositions; a person is not going to undertake to learn anything they think they already know.[189]

—Epictetus

Natural ability without training is blind.[190]

—Plutarch

It is not the man who has too little who is poor, but the one who hankers after more. What difference does it make how much there is laid away in a man's safe or in his barns, how many head of stock he grazes or how much capital he puts out at interest, if he is always after what is another's and only counts what he has yet to get, never what he has already. You ask what is the proper limit to a person's wealth? First, having what is essential, and second, having what is enough.[191]

—Seneca

We pursue beauty without extravagance and cultivate wisdom without being effete. We regard our wealth as a means for action and not as a reason to brag. No one sees poverty itself as shameful – the real shame lies in not taking steps to escape it.[192]

—Pericles

Don't hanker after what you don't have. Instead, fix your attentions on the finest and best that you have, and imagine how much you would long for these if they weren't in your possession. At the same time, don't become so attached to these things that you would be distraught if you were to lose them.[193]

—Marcus Aurelius

I deeply believe that leaders, whatever their profession, are wrong to allow distinctions of rank to flourish within their organizations. Living together on equal terms helps people develop deeper bonds and creates a common conscience.[194]

—Xenophon

There are two things that must be rooted out in human beings – arrogant opinion and mistrust. Arrogant opinion expects that there is nothing further needed, and mistrust assumes that under the torrent of circumstances there can be no happiness.[195]

—Epictetus

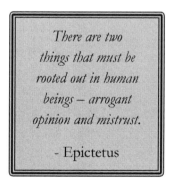

*There are two things that must be rooted out in human beings – arrogant opinion and mistrust.*

- Epictetus

Success should never breed complacency.[196]

—Xenophon

In the ashes all men are leveled. We're born unequal, we die equal.[197]

 —Seneca

All arrogance will reap a harvest rich in tears.
God calls men to a heavy reckoning
For overweening pride.[198]

 —Aeschylus

BOOK 5

# JUSTICE

Of all the universal principles, none of them strike a nerve in our collective conscience as much as that of fairness and justice. When we witness or experience something unjust, it serves as a catalyst for action to right the wrong, protect the injured, and punish the offender.

In today's world, it is an unfortunate reality that too many people still face racism, sexism, and discrimination of all kinds. Take this opportunity to reflect on your own leadership and ask yourself: am I truly treating everyone equally and fairly? Am I meting out discipline appropriately? Does everyone have an equal opportunity to succeed? What beliefs do I have that are incompatible with fairness and justice? What systemic issues contribute to unfairness or injustice in my organization?

As leaders, we must have a finely tuned sense of what is just and recognize that our inaction on issues will often say as much as our actions.

Justice is a human concern.[199]
—Aristotle

We become just by doing just acts, temperate by doing temperate acts, brave by doing brave acts.[200]
—Aristotle

Practice justice in word and deed, and do not get in the habit of acting thoughtlessly about anything.[201]
—Pythagoras

> *It is never right to do wrong or to requite wrong with wrong, or when we suffer evil to defend ourselves by doing evil in return.*
>
> - Socrates

It is never right to do wrong or to requite wrong with wrong, or when we suffer evil to defend ourselves by doing evil in return.[202]
—Socrates

Injustice results as often from not doing as from doing.[203]
—Marcus Aurelius

It is the way that we behave in our dealings with other people that makes us just or unjust, and the way that we behave in the

face of danger accustoming ourselves to be timid or confident, that makes us brave or cowardly.[204]
　　—Aristotle

The just man is the least disturbed by passion, the unjust man the most highly disturbed.[205]
　　—Epicurus

The evil you do to others you may expect in return.[206]
　　—Publius Syrus

He who does wrong does wrong against himself. He who acts unjustly acts unjustly to himself, because he makes himself bad.[207]
　　—Marcus Aurelius

Being treated unjustly and acting unjustly are both evils.[208]
　　—Aristotle

Injustice is a kind of blasphemy. Nature designed rational beings for each other's sake: to help – not harm – one another, as they deserve. To transgress its will, then is to blaspheme against the oldest of the gods.[209]
　　—Marcus Aurelius

Yes, my dear Glaucon, great is the struggle, great indeed, not what men think it, between good and evil, to be a good man or a bad man: no exaltation from honors or riches or power or anything soever, no, not from poetry itself, is worthy to make us careless of justice and all other virtue.[210]
　　—Socrates

The justice that seeks nature's goal is a utilitarian pledge of men not to harm each other or be harmed.[211]
—Epicurus

Have I acted unselfishly? Then I have benefited. Hold fast to this thought, and keep up the good work.[212]
—Marcus Aurelius

From the different comes the fairest harmony.[213]
—Heraclitus, as quoted by Aristotle

Avoid injustice.[214]
—Cleobulus

So too it is easy to get angry – anyone can do that – or to give and spend money; but to feel or act towards the right person to the right extent at the right time for the right reason in the right way – that is not easy, and it is not everyone that can do it. Hence to do these things well is a rare, laudable and fine achievement.[215]
—Aristotle

People should associate with one another in such a way as not to make their friends enemies, but to render their enemies friends.[216]
—Pythagoras

If it's not right, don't do it. If it's not true, don't say it.[217]
—Marcus Aurelius

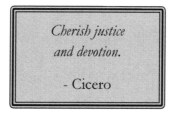

*Cherish justice
and devotion.*

- Cicero

Cherish justice and devotion. These qualities in abundance are owed to parents and kinsmen; and most of all they are owed to one's country.[218]

—Cicero

There is but one essential justice, which cements society, and one law which establishes this justice. This law is right reason, which is the true rule of all commandments and prohibitions. Whoever neglects this law, whether written or unwritten, is necessarily unjust and wicked.[219]

—Cicero

For man, when perfected, is the best of animals, but, when separated from law and justice, he is the worst of all; since armed injustice is the more dangerous, and he is equipped at birth with the arms of intelligence and with moral qualities which he may use for the worst ends. Wherefore, if he have not virtue, he is the most unholy and the most savage of animals, and the most full of lust and gluttony. But justice is the bond of men in states, and the administration of justice, which is the determination of what is just, is the principle of order in political society.[220]

—Aristotle

If the mind is common to us all, then so is reason that enables us to understand and tells us how to treat one another. If this is so, then we hold the law in common as well. We are fellow citizens, subject to one unwritten constitution, and the world is, as it were, a city. Indeed, what other citizenship is shared by the whole human race? From this common city, we derive mind, reason, and law, and if this is not so, where do they then come from?[221]

—Marcus Aurelius

Justice is the same thing as goodness, and the designation of a just man is bestowed upon the person whose character is untouched by any suspicion of dishonesty or unfair dealing – the sort of man to whom we should consider it safe to entrust our lives, our fortunes and our children. Goodness or justice is more effective than intelligence in inspiring trust. And indeed, even when intelligence is conspicuous by its absence, justice still carries great weight; whereas intelligence without justice creates no confidence at all. If a man is not regarded as honest, the more shrewd and sharp he is the more he will be disliked and distrusted. To sum up, then, a combination of justice and intelligence is best of all – and capable of winning all the confidence that could be desired. Justice without intelligence will also be able to achieve a great deal. But intelligence without justice is useless.[222]

—Cicero

People suppose that it is in their power to act unjustly, and that therefore it is easy to be just; but this is not so. To go to bed with your neighbor's wife, to strike the man next to you, to slip money into somebody's hand – this is easy and lies in their power; but it is not easy, nor in their power, to do these things as the outcome of a certain state of character. Similarly they assume that it takes no special wisdom to recognize what is just and unjust, because it is not difficult to understand the instructions that the law gives us (although the acts that it prescribes are just only incidentally);

but how actions are to be performed and distributions made in order to be just – to know that is a harder task.[223]

—Aristotle

"Whatever happens happens justly." Pay close attention and you will see that this is so. By this I don't mean only that justice will result from whatever happens, but I mean that a just process will also be served, as is the case when payment is made for work or prizes are awarded for victory. So be particularly scrupulous in this and continue as you have begun, a decent man, performing every deed conscious of the most rigorous requirements of goodness. Preserve this in every act.[224]

—Marcus Aurelius

Winning confidence...There are two requirements for this. A man must be considered intelligent; and he must be regarded as just. We feel confidence in people we believe to be wiser than ourselves, and better judges of the future – people who seem capable of dealing with critical situations and making whatever decisions circumstances require. For that is the sort of useful intelligence that people reckon to be the real thing.[225]

—Cicero

He sins who acts unjustly. All rational creatures, by nature's deep design and purpose, are created for one another. They are meant to help those who deserve help and in no way to harm one another. He who shrugs off the will of nature sins against the oldest of the gods.

He who tells lies sins against the same god. Nature is the basis for everything that is, and everything that is is intimately connected with everything that ever was. Truth is just another name for nature, the first cause of everything. He who lies with the intent of deceiving another sins by acting unjustly, but he who lies un-intentionally sins by striking a discordant note with nature and by opposing the profound harmony of the universe. By opposing truth, even unwittingly, the liar declares war on nature and loses through neglect his god-given ability to discern what is true and what is false.

He also sins who pursues pleasures as if they were good and flees hardships as if they were evil. Seeing how often evildoers enjoy pleasures and acquire things that bring pleasure while decent folk suffer hardships and encounter things that cause pain, this sort of person cannot help but blame nature for handing out pleasures and hardships indiscriminately. Moreover, the person afraid of hardship is at odds with something that is going to happen as part of the natural order of things, and this is sinful. Likewise, the person panting after pleasure will not hesitate to act unjustly, and this is clearly sinful.[226]

—Marcus Aurelius

> *He sins who acts unjustly. All rational creatures…are meant to help those who deserve help and in no way to harm one another.*
>
> - Marcus Aurelius

The ability to rise above outward circumstances, then, wins special admiration; and that is why justice, which is the peculiar mark of a good man, is universally regarded as marvelous. And quite right too. For if someone possesses this virtue, it means that he has emancipated himself from the fear of death and pain and exile and poverty: that is to say, he does not regard it as more important to achieve the reverses of these conditions than to behave like a decent person. And most of all people admire someone who refuses to be influenced by money. To prove oneself in that particular direction is the equivalent of emerging triumphantly from a fiery ordeal.[227]

—Cicero

So there is no doubt that the men chosen to rule in ancient times were those who enjoyed a great popular reputation for justice; and if they were believed to be intelligent as well, there was no limit to the advantages people expected to obtain under their leadership. But the main thing the leaders had to provide was justice. Indeed it is a quality that must be cultivated and maintained by every possible means. This must be done for its own sake – for that is what justice means, its very essence. But it is also true that just dealings add honor and glory to one's reputation.[228]

—Cicero

Justice in this sense, then, is complete virtue; virtue, however, not unqualified but in relation to somebody else. Hence it is often regarded as the sovereign virtue, and 'neither evening nor morning star is such a wonder.' We express it in a proverb: 'In justice is summed up the whole of virtue.' It is complete virtue in the fullest sense, because it is the active exercise of complete virtue; and it is complete because its possessor can exercise it in relation to another person, and not only by himself. I say this because there are plenty of people who can behave uprightly in their own affairs, but are incapable of doing so in relation to somebody else. That is why Bias' saying 'Office will reveal the man' is felt to be valid; because an official is *eo ipso* in a relation to, and associated with, somebody else. And for this same reason – that it implies a relation to somebody else – justice is the only virtue that is regarded as someone else's good, because it secures advantage for another person, either an official, or a partner. So the worst person is the one who exercises his wickedness towards both himself and his friends, and the best is not the one who exercises his virtue towards himself but the one who exercises it towards another; because this is a difficult task. Justice in this sense, then, is not a part of virtue but the whole of it, and the injustice contrary to it is not a part but the whole of vice.[229]

—Aristotle

> *Office will reveal the man...the best is not the one who exercises his virtue towards himself but the one who exercises it toward another; because this is a difficult task.*
>
> - Aristotle

It is impossible to live the pleasant life without also living sensibly, nobly, and justly, and conversely it is impossible to live sensibly, nobly, and justly without living pleasantly. A person who does not have a pleasant life is not living sensibly, nobly, and justly, and conversely the person who does not have these virtues cannot live pleasantly.[230]

—Epicurus

The most important consequence of just dealing is inner serenity.[231]

—Epicurus

For where might and justice are yoke-fellows – what pair is stronger than this?[232]

—Aeschylus

Life's one prize is in seeking truth and doing justice and being charitable even to those who lie and cheat.[233]

—Marcus Aurelius

You will not see that the likeliest way of securing peace is this: only to use one's power in the cause of justice, but to make it perfectly plain that one is resolved not to tolerate aggression. On the contrary, your idea of proper behavior is, firstly, to avoid harming others, and then to avoid being harmed yourselves, even if it is a matter of defending your own interests.[234]

—Thucydides

If you'd only let go of the past, entrust the future to Providence, and guide the present toward reverence and justice.

Reverence: so you'll accept what you're allotted. Nature intended it for you, and you for it.

Justice: so that you'll speak the truth, frankly and without evasions, and act as you should – and as other people deserve.[235]

—Marcus Aurelius

Never thrust upon another the burden you cannot carry yourself.[236]

—Publius Syrus

A lamp's flame throws light and does not lose its radiance until it is extinguished. Will the truth, justice, and wisdom within you die before your life is extinguished?[237]

—Marcus Aurelius

Those who really deserve praise are the people who, while human enough to enjoy power, nonetheless pay more attention to justice than they are compelled to do by their situation.[238]

—Thucydides

Why do you hesitate or second-guess yourself when you know perfectly well what ought to be done? If you know where you need to go, make a considerate but determined effort to get there. If you don't, wait and seek the best advice you can find. If you meet with resistance along the way, advance cautiously and prepare at any moment to take refuge in what you know to be just, for to reach your goal justly is the apotheosis of achievement whereas to advance even one inch by doing an injustice is the most miserable form of failure. Relaxed but alert, cheerful but determined—such is reason's faithful follower.[239]

—Marcus Aurelius

If you have the power to put a stop to subjugation, yet look the other way while it happens, then you have done it yourselves, more truly than if you had been the subjugators.[240]

—Thucydides

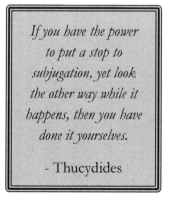

*If you have the power
to put a stop to
subjugation, yet look
the other way while it
happens, then you have
done it yourselves.*

- Thucydides

While those who mouth high talk
may think themselves high-minded,
justice keeps the book
on hypocrites and liars.[241]
　　—Heraclitus

Seek refuge in yourself. The knowledge of having acted justly is all your reasoning inner self needs to be fully content and at peace with itself.[242]
　　—Marcus Aurelius

Whether the universe is composed of an infinite number of blind atoms or one all-seeing nature, two things are clear: first, I am a part of the universe governed by nature; and second, I am related in some way to the other parts like myself. Once I acknowledge this, I shall be content with any role the universe assigns me, for nothing is bad for the part that is good for the whole, and the whole contains nothing which is not good for it. This is true for everything in nature, but the world has an additional safeguard: nothing from outside can interfere or force it to generate something harmful to itself.

Realizing that I am part of just such a universe, I will calmly accept whatever happens. And because I am related to the other parts like myself, I will not seek my own advantage at their expense, but I will study to know what is our common good and bend every effort to advance that good and to dissuade others from acting against it. If I am successful at this, my life is bound to flow smoothly, as one would expect for the dutiful citizen who is always looking out for others and enjoys whatever work his community asks of him.[243]

—Marcus Aurelius

BOOK 6

# COMMUNICATION

Communication is the glue that holds the world together and is the critical lynchpin to success in any organization.

When something goes well, effective communication was typically a key component. Similarly, when something goes wrong, at its core, it almost always started with a breakdown in communication.

Here are a few simple rules to remember about communication:

- Keep it simple. Communication should be clear and concise.
- Over-communicate. Good communication requires sustained, focused efforts.
- Know your audience. It's not only what you say or write, but how the people you are trying to communicate with receive your message.

As a leader, one of your foremost responsibilities is the Chief Communicator, don't neglect it.

A man who has the knowledge but lacks the power clearly to express it is no better off than if he never had any ideas at all.[244]

—Pericles

Better to trip with the feet than with the tongue.[245]

—Zeno

Whether speaking to the Senate or to the humblest person, use language that is respectful, but not affected. Let your speech be plain and honest.[246]

—Marcus Aurelius

In your conversation, don't dwell at excessive length on your own deeds or adventures. Just because you enjoy recounting your exploits doesn't mean that others derive the same pleasure from hearing about them.[247]

—Epictetus

A King does not slay a messenger.[248]

—Alexander the Great

Never say or do anything in anger.[249]

—Pythagoras

Now that is the first thing Socrates was known for – never turning dialogue into dispute, never introducing rudeness or invective, although he would put up with insults of others in order to avoid a fight. And if you want to know how effective he was, read Xenophon's *Symposium*; you will see how many fights he is credited there with resolving. Among the poets, too, one of the highest forms of compliment is one conveyed

in the line: He could cut short a quarrel, however great, with his diplomacy.[250]
—Epictetus

The reason why we have two ears and only one mouth is so we might listen more and talk less.[251]
—Zeno

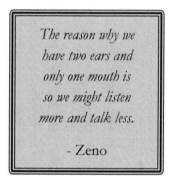

The reason why we have two ears and only one mouth is so we might listen more and talk less.

- Zeno

Be fond of hearing rather than of talking.[252]
—Cleobulus

Practice really hearing what people say. Do your best to get inside their minds.[253]
—Marcus Aurelius

Silent discretion is not found in years so inexperienced; perchance they will disclose the plot; the art of silence is taught by life's many ills.[254]
—Seneca

A multitude of words is no proof of a prudent mind.[255]
—Thales

It is better wither to be silent, or to say things of more value than silence. Sooner throw a pearl at hazard than an idle or useless word; and do not say a little in many words, but a great deal in a few.[256]

 —Pythagoras

Most people, in fact, will not take trouble in finding out the truth, but are much more inclined to accept the first story they hear.[257]

 —Thucydides

People dull their wits with gibberish,
and cannot use their ears and eyes.
Many fail to grasp what they have seen,
and cannot judge what they have learned,
although they tell themselves they know.
Yet they lack the skill
to listen or to speak.
Whoever cannot seek
The unforeseen sees nothing,
for the known way is an impasse.[258]

 —Heraclitus

The importance of every word depends on the sense you give it.[259]

 —Publius Syrus

Brevity is the soul of command.[260]

 —Xenophon

Far and away the best creator of eloquence is the pen.[261]

 —Cicero

When we really put a great deal of work and concentration into a speech, then, after that, all the arguments we could possibly need for what we want to say, arguments derived either from our studies or from the natural workings of our intelligence, will automatically surge forward and present themselves all ready for our use. That is how to make all the most brilliant thoughts and expressions crowd on to the point of our pen. And that, too, is the way to ensure that every single word is located and arranged in its proper place, according to the particularly rhythmical scheme which is appropriate to oratory as opposed to poetry.[262]

—Cicero

Admonish your friends in private; praise them in public.[263]

—Publius Syrus

People often say what is right and do what is wrong; but nobody can be in the wrong if he is doing what is right.[264]

—Hippias

There is a class of men who communicate, to anyone whom they meet, matters which should be revealed to friends alone, and unload upon the chance listener whatever irks them. Others, again, fear to confide in their closest intimates; and if it were possible, they would not trust even themselves, burying their secrets deep in their hearts. But we should do neither. It is equally faulty to trust everyone and to trust no one.[265]

—Seneca

Why do we not hear the truth? Because we don't speak it.[266]

—Publius Syrus

> *For the lover of truth,*
> *who speaks it when*
> *nothing depends on it,*
> *will speak it all the*
> *more when something*
> *does depend on it.*
>
> - Aristotle

Falsehood is in itself bad and reprehensible, while the truth is a fine and praiseworthy thing...for the lover of the truth, who speaks it when nothing depends upon it, will speak it all the more when something does depend on it.[267]

—Aristotle

Many words befall men, mean and noble alike; do not be astonished by them, nor allow yourself to be constrained. If a lie is told, bear with it gently. But whatever I tell you, let it be done completely. Let no one persuade you by word or deed to do or say whatever is not best for you.[268]

—Pythagoras

Pay close attention in conversation to what is being said, and to what follows from any action. In any action, immediately look for the target, in words, listen closely to what's being signaled.[269]

—Marcus Aurelius

When any alarming news is brought you, always have it ready in mind that no news can be brought you concerning what is within the power of your own Will. Can anyone bring you news that your opinions or desires are ill conducted? By no means; only [to say] that such a person is dead. What is that to you then? That somebody speaks ill of you. And what is that to you then...why do you any longer trouble yourself about it? [270]

—Epictetus

When we speak evil of others, we generally condemn ourselves.[271]

—Publius Syrus

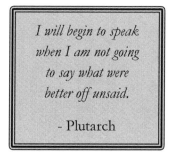

> *I will begin to speak when I am not going to say what were better off unsaid.*
>
> - Plutarch

Cato practiced also the kind of speaking which is effective with a multitude, deeming it right that in political philosophy, as in a great city, a certain warlike element should also be maintained. However, he did not perform his exercises in company with others, nor did anyone ever hear him rehearsing a speech. Indeed, to one of his companions who said, "Men find fault with thee, Cato, for thy silence," he replied: "Only let them not blame my life. I will begin to speak when I am not going to say what were better off unsaid."[272]

—Plutarch

You will be doing the right thing, therefore, if you do not go to listen to people who are more concerned about the quantity than the quality of what they say.[273]

—Seneca

Settle on the type of person you want to be and stick to it, whether alone or in company. Let silence be your goal for the most part; say only what is necessary, and be brief about it. On the rare occasions when you're called upon to speak, then speak, but never about banalities like gladiators, horses, sports, food and drink – commonplace stuff. Above all don't gossip about people, praising, blaming or comparing them. Try to influence your friends to speak appropriately by your example.[274]

    —Epictetus

Many words were said by Plato, said by Zeno, said by Chrysippus and Posidonius and a whole host more of Stoics like them. Let me indicate here how men can prove that their words are their own: let them put their preaching into practice.[275]

    —Seneca

Forge thy tongue on an anvil of truth
And what flies up, though it may be but a spark,
Shall have weight.[276]

    —Pindar

Hateful to me as the gates of Hades is the man who hides one thing in his heart and speaks another.[277]

    —Homer

I count false words the foulest plague of all.[278]

    —Aeschylus

> *I count false words the*
> *foulest plague of all.*
>
> - Aeschylus

BOOK 7

# JUDGMENT

Many of the ancient philosophers understood the importance of thoughtfulness and judgment. To them, it was essential to reflect, to separate emotion from decision-making, and to use your judgment in pursuit of some higher purpose.

Nowadays the judgment and decisions of a leader, amplified by news and social media, can sway the entire trajectory of an organization in a nanosecond. As such, it is critical that you build time into your schedule to reflect, to think, and to decide. Only then will you be able to make the best judgments regarding people, risk, and long-term plans. And remember, it's okay to change your past judgments and opinions when presented with new information.

Reason and calm judgment, the qualities specially belonging to a leader.[279]

—Tacitus

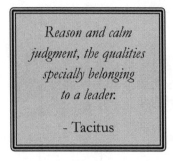

*Reason and calm judgment, the qualities specially belonging to a leader.*

- Tacitus

These are the characteristics of the rational soul: self-awareness, self-examination, and self-determination. It reaps its own harvest...It reaches its intended goal...Also characteristics of the rational soul: Affection for its neighbors. Truthfulness. Humility. Not to place anything above itself.[280]

—Marcus Aurelius

Truly, men often fail to understand their own weaknesses, and their lack of self-knowledge can bring terrible disasters down on their own heads.[281]

—Xenophon

Apply reason to difficulties; it is possible to soften what is hard, to widen what is narrow, and burdens will press less heavily upon those who bear them skillfully.[282]

—Seneca

You breathe the air that surrounds you. Why not think with the intelligence that surrounds everything? No less than the air we

breathe, the power to think pervades everything and flows to those who draw upon it.[283]
—Marcus Aurelius

To be everywhere is to be nowhere.[284]
—Seneca

An arrow flies one way, a thought another. Yet a thought, when it is aimed with care and circumspection, speeds to its target no less directly.[285]
—Marcus Aurelius

The proper work of the mind is the exercise of choice, refusal, yearning, repulsion, preparation, purpose, and assent. What then can pollute and clog the mind's proper functioning? Nothing but its own corrupt decisions.[286]
—Epictetus

Most of what we say and do is unnecessary anyway; subtract all that lot, and look at the time and contentment you'll gain. On each occasion, therefore, a man should ask himself, "Do I really need to say or do this?" In this way, he will remove not only unnecessary actions, but also the superfluous ideas that inspire needless acts.[287]
—Marcus Aurelius

Don't try to cover your mistakes with false words. Rather, correct your mistakes with examination.[288]
—Pythagoras

> *Don't try to cover your mistakes with false words. Rather, correct your mistakes with examination.*
>
> - Pythagoras

The matter can be imparted quickly and in very few words: Virtue is the only good; at any rate there is no good without virtue; and virtue itself is situated in our nobler part, that is, the rational part. And what will this virtue be? A true and never-swerving judgment. For therefrom will spring all mental impulses, and by its agency every external appearance that stirs our impulses will be clarified.[289]

—Seneca

When forced, as it seems, by circumstances into utter confusion, get a hold of yourself quickly. Don't be locked out of rhythm any longer than necessary. You'll be able to keep the beat if you are constantly returning to it.[290]

—Marcus Aurelius

A hasty judgment is a first step to a recantation.[291]

—Publius Syrus

I think the two biggest obstacles to good decision-making are haste and anger. The first tends to go hand in hand with foolishness, the second with recklessness and snap judgments.[292]

—Diodotus

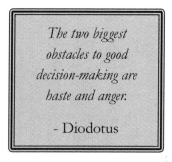

*The two biggest obstacles to good decision-making are haste and anger.*

- Diodotus

The first thing to do – don't get worked up. For everything happens according to the nature of all things, and in a short time you'll be nobody and nowhere, even as the great emperors Hadrian and Augustus are now. The next thing to do – consider carefully the task at hand for what it is, while remembering that your purpose is to be a good human being. Get straight to doing what nature requires of you, and speak as you see most just and fitting – with kindness, modesty, sincerity.[293]

　—Marcus Aurelius

Don't trust in your reputation, money, or position, but in the strength that is yours – namely, your judgments about the things that you control and don't control. For this alone is what makes us free and unfettered, that picks us up by the neck from the depths and lifts us eye to eye with the rich and powerful.[294]

　—Epictetus

You take things you don't control and define them as "good" and "bad." And so of course when the "bad" things happen, or the "good ones don't, you blame the gods and feel hatred for the people responsible – or those you decide to make responsible. Much of our bad behavior stems from trying to apply those criteria. If we limited "good" and "bad" to our own actions,

we'd have no call to challenge God, or to treat other people as enemies.[295]
—Marcus Aurelius

Thus our judgments, if they do not borrow from reason and philosophy a fixity and steadfastness of purpose in their acts, are easily swayed and influenced by the praise or blame of others, which make us distrust our own opinions.[296]
—Plutarch

Everywhere, at each moment, you have the option:
- to accept this event with humility
- to treat this person as he should be treated
- to approach this thought with care, so that nothing irrational creeps in.[297]

—Marcus Aurelius

Who are you? In the first place, a human being, which is to say, a being possessed of no greater faculty than free choice, with all your other faculties subordinate to it, choice itself being unconfined and independent. Next, consider the gift of reason: it sets you apart from the wild animals; it sets you apart from sheep. By virtue of these two faculties you are a member of the universe with full citizen rights; you were born not to serve but to govern. Now, what does the title 'citizen' mean? In this role a person never acts in his own interest or thinks of himself alone, but, like a hand or foot that had sense and realized its place in the natural order, all its actions and desires aim at nothing except contributing to the common good.[298]
—Epictetus

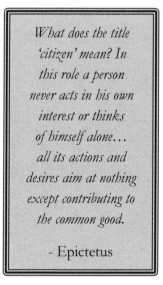

*What does the title 'citizen' mean? In this role a person never acts in his own interest or thinks of himself alone... all its actions and desires aim at nothing except contributing to the common good.*

- Epictetus

The eye, the ear,
the mind in action,
these I value.[299]
    —Heraclitus

...The soul never thinks without an image.[300]
    —Aristotle.

When you are distressed by an external thing, it's not the thing itself that troubles you, but only your judgment of it. And you can wipe this out at a moment's notice.[301]
    —Marcus Aurelius

The soul of man is divided into three parts, intelligence, reason, and passion. Intelligence and passion are possessed by other animals, but reason by man alone.[302]
    —Pythagoras

Does the news bother you? Do you worry about things out of your control? Then take the time to concentrate your mind in the acquisition of some new and useful knowledge and stop it from flitting about. By the same token, guard against making the mistake of those who keep themselves so busy trying to gain control that they wear themselves out and lose their sense of direction having no purpose to guide their actions or even their thoughts.[303]

—Marcus Aurelius

Just keep in mind: the more we value things outside our control, the less control we have.[304]

—Epictetus

If your body was turned over to just anyone, you would doubtless take exception. Why aren't you ashamed that you have made your mind vulnerable to anyone who happens to criticize you, so that it automatically becomes confused and upset?[305]

—Epictetus

Everything turns on your assumptions about it, and that's on you. You can pluck out the hasty judgment at will, and like steering a ship around the point, you will find calm seas, fair weather, and a safe port.[306]

—Marcus Aurelius

Now the origin of action is choice, and the origin of choice is appetition and purposive reasoning. Hence choice necessarily involves not only intellect and thought, but a certain moral state; for good conduct and its contrary necessarily involve thought and character. But no process is set going by mere thought – only by purposive and practical thought, for it is this that also originates productive thought.[307]

—Aristotle

> *The origin of action is choice, and the origin of choice is appetition and purposive reasoning.*
>
> - Aristotle

Test every thought and sense perception, if possible, by the methods of science, the laws of morality, and the rules of logic.[308]

—Marcus Aurelius

The power to live an exemplary life resides in the mind, so long as the mind remains indifferent to the things that are themselves indifferent. But how can it remain indifferent? By carefully examining each thing, both as a whole and in its parts, and by remembering that nothing can oblige us to form an opinion of it. Things don't force themselves upon us. They stand still, while we form judgments of them and write them down, so to speak, on our minds.[309]

—Marcus Aurelius

Look always at the whole. What is it that has made this impression on your senses? Analyze it by breaking it down into cause, matter, purpose, and duration.[310]

—Marcus Aurelius

In everything you see someone else do, make it a habit to ask yourself, "What is his purpose in doing this?" But begin with yourself. Question your own actions first.[311]

—Marcus Aurelius

Never praise or blame people on common grounds; look to their judgments exclusively. Because that is the determining factor, which makes everyone's actions either good or bad.[312]

—Epictetus

So when we are frustrated, angry or unhappy, never hold anyone except ourselves – that is, our judgments – accountable. An ignorant person is inclined to blame others for his own misfortune. To blame oneself is proof of progress. But the wise man never has to blame another or himself.[313]

—Epictetus

We should discipline ourselves in small things, and from there progress to things of greater value.[314]

—Epictetus

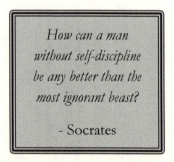

*How can a man without self-discipline be any better than the most ignorant beast?*

- Socrates

How can a man without self-discipline be any better than the most ignorant beast? If a person doesn't consider what is best, but tries by every means to do what is most pleasant, how can he be any better than the most senseless animals? Only the self-disciplined have the capacity to consider what are the best objects of action and, by both theoretically and practically categorizing good and bad, to choose the former and abstain from the latter.[315]

—Socrates

It is not events that disturb people, it is their judgments about them.[316]

—Epictetus

The things you think about determine the quality of your mind. Your soul takes on the color of your thoughts.[317]

—Marcus Aurelius

The body is the raw material of the doctor and physical therapist. Land is the farmer's raw material. The raw material of the good man is his mind – his goal being to respond to impressions the way nature intended. As a general rule, nature designed the mind to assent to what is true, dissent from what is false and suspend judgment in doubtful cases. Similarly, it conditioned the mind to desire what is good, to reject what is bad and to regard with indifference what is neither one nor the other.[318]

—Epictetus

The mind has to be given some time off, but in such a way that it may be refreshed, not relaxed till it goes to pieces.[319]

—Seneca

Do not waste the rest of your life speculating about others in ways that are not to your mutual advantage. Think of all that might be accomplished in the time you throw away – distracted from the voice of your own true and reasonable self-wondering what the next man is up to and why, what's he saying, or thinking, or plotting. Purge your mind of all aimless and idle thoughts, especially those that pry into the affairs of others or wish them ill. Get in the habit of limiting yourself only to those that – if you are suddenly asked, "What are you thinking at this moment?" – enable you to reply without equivocation or hesitation, "This" or "That." In this way, you show the world a simple and kindly man, a good neighbor, someone who is indifferent to sensual pleasures and luxuries and untouched by jealously, envy, mistrust, or any other thought you would blush to admit.[320]

—Marcus Aurelius

A friend of mine arbitrarily decided that he was going to starve himself to death. When I heard that he was already three days into his fast, I went and asked him to explain.

'I made my decision,' he said.

'Yes, but what drove you to it? Look, if it is the right decision, we are ready to sit by your side and help you make the passage. But if it was a reckless decision, it should be open to change.'

'But we must stick with a decision.'

'For heaven's sake, man, that rule only applies to sound decisions. I suppose next you will decide that it is night now, and refuse to change your mind because you don't want to. You will repeat, "We must stick with a decision." Begin with a firm foundation; evaluate your decision to see if it is valid – then there will be a basis for this rigid resolve of yours. If your foundation is rotten or crumbling, not a thing should be built on it, and the bigger and grander you make it, the sooner it will collapse.'[321]

—Epictetus

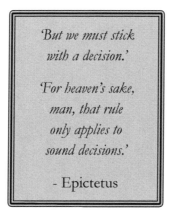

'But we must stick
with a decision.'

'For heaven's sake,
man, that rule
only applies to
sound decisions.'

- Epictetus

Impressions come to us in four ways: things are and appear to be; or they are not, and do not appear to be; or they are, but do not appear to be, or they are not, and yet appear to be. The duty of an educated man in all these cases is to judge correctly. And whatever disturbs our judgment, for that we need to find a solution.[322]
—Epictetus

Everyone dreams of the perfect vacation—in the country, by the sea, or in the mountains. You too long to get away and find that idyllic spot yet how foolish...when at any time you are capable of finding that perfect vacation in yourself. Nowhere is there a more idyllic spot, a vacation home more private and peaceful, than in one's own mind, especially when it is furnished in such a way that the merest inward glance induces ease (and by ease I mean the effects of an orderly and well-appointed mind, neither lavish nor crude). Take this vacation as often as you like, and so charge your spirit. But do not prolong these meditative moments beyond what is necessary to send you back to your work free of anxiety and full of vigor and good cheer.[323]
—Marcus Aurelius

You can take it from me that there is no other feat of endurance either – in fact there is no activity of any kind – in which you will be at a disadvantage from having your body better prepared. The body is valuable for all human activities, and in all its uses it is very important that it should be as fit as possible. Even in the act of thinking, which is supposed to require least assistance from the body, everyone knows that serious mistakes often happen through physical ill-health. Many people's minds are often so invaded by forgetfulness, despondency, irritability and insanity because of their poor physical condition that their knowledge is actually driven out of them.[324]

—Xenophon

It is inevitable if you enter into relations with people on a regular basis, either for conversation, dining or simple friendship, that you will grow to be like them, unless you can get them to emulate you. Place an extinguished piece of coal next to a live one, and either it will cause the other one to die out, or the live one will make the other reignite. Since a lot is at stake, you should be careful about fraternizing with non-philosophers in these contexts; remember that if you consort with someone covered in dirt you can hardly avoid getting a little grimy yourself.[325]

—Epictetus

> *Remember that if you consort with someone covered in dirt you can hardly avoid getting a little grimy yourself.*
>
> - Epictetus

If you are looking on anyone as a friend when you do not trust him as you trust yourself, you are making a grave mistake, and have failed to grasp sufficiently the full force of true friendship... After friendship is formed you must trust, but before that you must judge. Those people who, contrary to Theophrastus' advice, judge a man after they have made him their friend instead of the other way round, certainly put the cart before the horse. Think for a long time whether or not you should admit a given person to your friendship.[326]

—Seneca

Nobody will keep the things he hears to himself, and nobody will repeat just what he hears and no more. Neither will anyone who has failed to keep a story to himself keep the name of his informant to himself. Every person without exception has someone to whom he confides everything that is confided to himself.[327]

—Seneca

We strive to be daring and reflective in our planning.[328]

—Pericles

I think that those who exercise reason and believe that they are capable of teaching their fellow citizens what is for their good are most unlikely to become unruly, since they know that violence involves enmity and danger, whereas persuasion produces the same results without danger and in a friendly spirit; for the victims of violence feel that they have been deprived, and are resentful, while those who have yielded to persuasion are appreciative of having received a kindness. So violence is not to be expected of those who exercise reason; such conduct belongs to those who have strength without judgment.[329]

—Xenophon

In the end, what would you gain from everlasting remembrance? Absolutely nothing. So what is left worth living for? This alone: justice in thought, goodness in action, speech that cannot deceive, and a disposition glad of whatever comes, welcoming it as necessary, as familiar, as flowing from the same source and fountain as yourself.[330]

—Marcus Aurelius

It is necessary to take into account both the actual goal of life and the whole body of clear and distinct percepts to which we refer our judgments. If we fail to do this, everything will be in disorder and confusion. If you reject all sensations, you will not have any point of reference by which to judge even the ones you claim are false.

If you summarily rule out any single sensation and do not make a distinction between the element of belief that is superimposed on a percept that awaits verification and what is actually present in sensation or in the feelings or some percept of the mind itself, you will cast doubt on all other sensations by your unfounded interpretation and consequently abandon all the criteria of truth. On the other hand, in cases of interrupted data, if you accept as true those that need verification as well as those that do not, you will still be in error, since the whole question at issue in every judgment of what is true or not true will be left intact.

If at any time you fail to refer each of your acts to nature's standard, and turn off instead in some other direction when making a choice to avoid or pursue, your actions will not be consistent with your creed.[331]

—Epicurus

Make it your goal never to fail in your desires or experience things you would rather avoid; try never to err in impulse and repulsion; aim to be perfect also in the practice of attention and withholding judgment.[332]

—Epictetus

We must put the following question to each of our desires: What will happen to me if the object of my desire is achieved? What will happen if it is not?[333]

—Epicurus

Free from passions, the mind is a veritable fortress.[334]

—Marcus Aurelius

The self-controlled man alone will know himself and be able to examine what he in fact knows and what he doesn't, and he will be capable of looking at other people in the same way to see what any of them knows and thinks he knows, if he does know; and what, on the other hand, he thinks he knows, but does not. No one else will be able to do that. In fact, that is being self-controlled and self-control and knowing oneself – knowing what one knows and what one doesn't.[335]

—Socrates

Blot out imagination; restrain impulse; stifle desire; give your reason the upper hand.[336]

—Marcus Aurelius

In every one of us there are two guiding and ruling principles which leads us whither they will; one is the natural desire of pleasure, the other is an acquired judgment which aspires after excellence; and these two are sometimes in harmony and then

again at war, and sometimes the one, sometimes the other con-
quers. When opinion by the help of reason leads us to the best,
the conquering principle is called temperance; but when desire,
which is devoid of reason, rules in us and drags us to pleasure,
that power of misrule is called excess.[337]

 —Socrates

Some desires are (1) natural and necessary, others (2) natural
but not necessary, still others (3) neither natural nor necessary
but generated by senseless whims. All desires that do not lead to
physical pain if not satisfied are unnecessary, and involve cravings
that are easily resolved when they appear to entail harm or when
the object of desire is hard to get.

If interest is intense in the case of those natural desires that do
not lead to physical pain when they are not satisfied, then such
desires are generated by idle fancy, and it is not because of their
own nature that they are not dissipated but because of the person's own senseless whims.[338]

 —Epicurus

Treat with utmost respect your power of forming opinions, for
this power alone guards you against making assumptions that are
contrary to nature and judgments that overthrow the rule of reason. It enables you to learn from experience, to live in harmony
with others, and to walk in the way of the gods.[339]

 —Marcus Aurelius

It is better said Socrates, to change an opinion, than to persist in
a wrong one.[340]

 —Xenophon

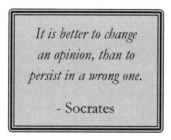

*It is better to change
an opinion, than to
persist in a wrong one.*

- Socrates

Remember that you don't lose any freedom by changing your mind and accepting the correction of someone who points out your error. After all, it's your initiative, your judgment, indeed your intelligence that makes change and acceptance possible.[341]

—Marcus Aurelius

There is one road to peace and happiness (keep the thought near by morning, noon and night): renunciation of externals; regarding nothing as your own; handing over everything to fortune and the deity.[342]

—Epictetus

Whatever you do, don't be troubled or anxious, but be free, and look at things like a human being, a citizen, a part of the creation that must die. Chief among the thoughts close at hand, keep these two: first, that nothing outside the mind can disturb it—trouble comes from the mind's opinion of what lies outside it; and second, that everything you now see will change in a moment and soon be no more.[343]

—Marcus Aurelius

The mind, to think of the accord
that strains against itself,
needs strength, as does the arm

to string the bow or lyre.
From the strain
of binding opposites
comes harmony.
The harmony past knowing sounds
more deeply than the known.
Yet let's not make
rash guesses
our most lucid thoughts.
Seekers of wisdom first
need sound intelligence.[344]
    —Heraclitus

The quality that we call self-sufficiency will belong in the highest degree to the contemplative activity. The wise man, no less than the just one and all the rest, requires the necessaries of life; but, given an adequate supply of these, the just man also needs people with and towards whom he can perform just actions, and similarly with the temperate man, the brave man and each of the others; but the wise man can practice contemplation by himself, and the wiser he is, the more he can do it.[345]
    —Aristotle

Objective judgment, now, at this moment.
Unselfish action, now, at this very moment.
Willing acceptance – now, at this very moment – of all external events.
That's all you need.[346]
    —Marcus Aurelius

You always own the option of having no opinions. There is never any need to get worked up or to trouble your soul about things you can't control. These things are not asking to be judged by you. Leave them alone.[347]

—Marcus Aurelius

Is my mind up to this task or not? If it is, I shall use it to do the work as one would a tool supplied by nature. If not, I will leave the job to someone better able to accomplish it, or if that is not possible, I will do it as best I can with the help of someone who, with my guidance and support, can complete a timely and useful work for the community. But in whatever I do, whether on my own or with someone else, my one objective will be this and only this: to benefit and to live in harmony with the community.[348]

—Marcus Aurelius

Make haste to examine your own mind, the mind of the universe, and the mind of your neighbor. Your own mind to make sure it is just. The mind of the universe to remind yourself of what you are a part. Your neighbor's mind to figure out whether he acted knowingly or out of ignorance and while doing this to reflect that he is your brother.[349]

—Marcus Aurelius

Do not let sleep close your tired eyes until you have gone over the day three times in your mind. What did I do wrong? What did I accomplish? What did I fail to do that I should have done? Starting from the beginning, go through to the end. Then, reproach yourself for the things you did wrong, and take pleasure in the good things you did.[350]

—Pythagoras

> *Do not let sleep close*
> *your tired eyes until*
> *you have gone over*
> *the day three times*
> *in your mind.*
>
> - Pythagoras

To these truths add one more: whenever you see or imagine something, make a precise mental picture of it, stripped to its bare essence and divorced from its surroundings; call it by its proper name, and name each of the parts that compose it and into which it will someday decompose. Nothing produces greatness of mind like the habit of examining methodically and honestly everything we encounter in this life and of determining its place in the order of things, its intended use, its value to the whole universe, and its worth to man in his role as citizen of that world City in which all other cities are but households.[351]

—Marcus Aurelius

Unexpectedness adds to the weight of a disaster. The fact that it was unforeseen has never failed to intensify a person's grief. This is a reason for ensuring that nothing ever takes us by surprise. We should project our thoughts ahead of us at every turn and have in mind every possible eventuality instead of only the usual course of events.[352]

—Seneca

In short, you must remember this – that if you hold anything dear outside of your own reasoned choice, you will have destroyed your capacity for choice.[353]

—Epictetus

Above all, the search after truth and its eager pursuit are peculiar to man.[354]

—Cicero

*To what service is my soul committed? Constantly ask yourself this and thoroughly examine yourself.*

- Marcus Aurelius

To what service is my soul committed? Constantly ask yourself this and thoroughly examine yourself by seeing how you relate to that part called the ruling principle...[355]

—Marcus Aurelius

BOOK 8

# ACTION

In the military there is a saying: "A good decision now, is better than a great decision later." From a recruit's first days in basic military training, this principle is drilled into them; no matter the situation, you must assess the information you have, decide, and act. If you do this faster than the adversary, you win; if you don't, you lose.

Similarly, the ancient philosophers believed two key and counter-balancing ideas about action. The first was the notion of seizing the opportunity each day and not letting time pass you by. If there was ever a question regarding whether to act or not act, they heavily favored the former. Second, they cautioned that there was great danger in just acting carelessly, without purpose, not in accordance with our "right principle" (our values), or before the likely consequences are understood. Action was important, but so too was thoughtful judgment, and you cannot have one without the other.

While it is important to understand that acting may lead to mistakes and failures, failing to act can be even more detrimental. When in doubt, have a bias for action.

Men who are capable of real action first make their plans and then go forward without hesitation while their enemies have still not made up their minds.[356]

—Thucydides

> *Men who are capable of real action first make their plans and then go forward without hesitation while their enemies have still not made up their minds.*
>
> - Thucydides

Seize the unexpected opportunity.[357]

—Xenophon

Act, speak, and think like a man ready to depart this life in the next breath.[358]

—Marcus Aurelius

I judge by deeds, not words.[359]

—Aeschylus

Before you act, ask yourself: "What are the likely consequences of this act? Will I later have cause to regret it?"[360]

—Marcus Aurelius

We do not think that there is an incompatibility between words and deeds; the worst thing is to rush into action before the consequences have been properly debated.[361]
—Thucydides

Sound thinking
is to listen well and choose
one course of action.[362]
—Heraclitus

We should act according to the right principle.[363]
—Aristotle

First, do nothing unintentionally or without some end in mind. Second, make the common good the only end of all your actions.[364]
—Marcus Aurelius

The very best deeds are those which serve your country.[365]
—Cicero

Every man who has preserved or helped his country, or has made its greatness even greater, is reserved a special place in heaven, where he may enjoy an eternal life of happiness.[366]
—Cicero

The end...is not knowledge, but action.[367]
—Aristotle

First, tell yourself what you want to be, then act your part accordingly. This, after all, is what we find to be the rule in just about every other field. Athletes decide first what they want to be, then proceed to do what is necessary. If they decide to be a distance runner, it means one particular diet, racecourse, workout and mode of physical therapy. If they want to be sprinters, those factors are different. And if it's a pentathlete they want to be, they vary again. You will find the same thing true of the crafts. If you want to be a carpenter, you will have one kind of training, if you want to be a sculptor, quite another. All our efforts must be directed towards an end, or we will act in vain. If it is not the right end, we will fail utterly.[368]

—Epictetus

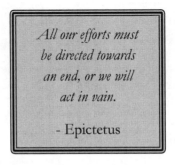

*All our efforts must be directed towards an end, or we will act in vain.*

*- Epictetus*

There are in the soul three things that control action and the attainment of truth, namely sensation, intellect and appetition... now the origin of action is choice, and the origin of choice is appetition and purposive reasoning.[369]

—Aristotle

How to act:

Never under compulsion, out of selfishness, without forethought, with misgivings.

Don't gussy up your thoughts.

No surplus words or unnecessary actions.

Let the spirit in you represent a man, an adult, a citizen, a Roman, a ruler. Taking up his post like a soldier and patiently awaiting his recall from life. Needing no oath or witness.

Cheerfulness. Without requiring other people's help. Or serenity supplied by others.
To stand up straight – not straightened.[370]
—Marcus Aurelius

I, for my part, think that to a brave man, there is no end to labors except the labors themselves...[371]
—Alexander the Great

Nothing that is really good and admirable is granted by the gods to men without some effort and application.[372]
—Xenophon

Let us therefore set out whole-heartedly, leaving aside our many distractions and exert ourselves in this single purpose, before we realize too late the swift and unstoppable flight of time and are left behind. As each day rises, welcome it as the very best day of all, and make it your own possession. We must seize what flees.[373]
—Seneca

> *As each day rises,*
> *welcome it as the very*
> *best day of all, and*
> *make it your own*
> *possession. We must*
> *seize what flees.*
>
> - Seneca

You should stop wasting time on things that bring no benefits to you.[374]
—Aeschylus

No work is shame, but idleness is shame.[375]
—Hesiod

Work is the sustenance of noble minds.[376]
—Seneca

The whole life of man is but a point of time; let us enjoy it, therefore, while it lasts, and not spend it to no purpose.[377]
—Plutarch

People who labor all their lives but have no purpose to direct every thought and impulse toward are wasting their time – even when hard at work.[378]
—Marcus Aurelius

It is hard to recover the lost opportunity.[379]
—Publius Syrus

Every day should be passed as if it were to be our last.[380]
—Publius Syrus

Any day stands
equal to the rest.
One's bearing
shapes one's fate.[381]
—Heraclitus

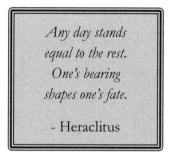

*Any day stands
equal to the rest.
One's bearing
shapes one's fate.*

- Heraclitus

Life without ideals is erratic: as soon as an ideal is to be set up, doctrines begin to be necessary. I am sure you will admit that there is nothing more shameful than uncertain and wavering conduct, than the habit of cowardly retreat. This will be our experience in all cases unless we remove that which checks the spirit and clogs it, and keeps it from making an attempt and trying with all its might. [382]

 —Seneca

Let all your efforts be directed to something, let it keep that end in view. It's not activity that disturbs people, but false conceptions of things that drive them mad.[383]

 —Seneca

True good fortune is what you make for yourself. Good fortune: good character, good intentions, good actions.[384]

 —Marcus Aurelius

Every habit and faculty is maintained and increased by its corresponding actions: the habit of walking by walking, the habit of running by running. If you would be a good reader, read; if a writer, write. But when you shall not have read for thirty days in succession, but have done something else, you will know the consequence. In the same way, if you shall have lain down ten

days, get up and attempt to make a long walk, and you will see how your legs are weakened. Generally then if you would make anything a habit, do it; if you would not make it a habit, do not do it, but accustom yourself to do something else in place of it.[385]
  —Epictetus

Nothing is stronger than habit.[386]
  —Ovid

Show them by your actions.[387]
  —Epictetus

All things move and nothing remains still.[388]
  —Heraclitus, as quoted by Plato

Over-analysis breeds hesitation to act.[389]
  —Pericles

Do human beings in general attain to well-tempered manhood by a course of idling or by carefully attending to what will be of use? Which will help a man the more to grow in justice and uprightness, to be up and doing, or to sit with folded hands revolving the ways and means of existence?[390]
  —Socrates

At dawn, when you have trouble getting out of bed, tell yourself: "I have to go to work – as a human being. What do I have to complain of, if I'm going to do what I was born for – the things I was brought into the world to do? Or is this what I was created for? To huddle under the blankets and stay warm?"[391]
  —Marcus Aurelius

Just as at the Olympic Games it is not the best-looking or the strongest men present that are crowded with wreaths, but the competitors (because it is from them that the winners come), so it is those who *act* that rightly win the honors and rewards in life.[392]

—Aristotle

Try to persuade others and bring them along, but act, whether they like it or not, whenever reason or justice demands. If they throw up barriers or use force to stop you, remain calm and welcome their opposition as an opportunity to practice the virtues of patience and self-control. Remember that your abilities to reason and to discern right from wrong are not infallible and that you are not called upon to do the impossible. What is expected from you? The very actions you have taken. By taking them, you have reached your goal and achieved your purpose. Know that in time those things toward which we move come to be.[393]

—Marcus Aurelius

> *Try to persuade others*
> *and bring them along,*
> *but act, whether*
> *they like it or not,*
> *whenever reason or*
> *justice demands.*
>
> - Marcus Aurelius

Just as Calypso advises: 'Far from this surf and surge keep thou thy ship.' For one of the extremes is always more erroneous than the other; and since it is extremely difficult to hit the mean, we must take the next best course, as they say, and choose the lesser of the evils.[394]

—Aristotle

If you decide to do something, don't shrink from being seen doing it, even if the majority of people disapprove. If you're wrong to do it, then you should shrink from doing it altogether; but if you're right, then why worry how people will judge you?[395]

—Epictetus

When facing whatever happens outside your control, be calm; when taking actions for which you are responsible, be fair. In other words, whether acting or reacting, your aim is the aid and betterment of others, in fulfilment of nature's laws.[396]

—Marcus Aurelius

But the virtues we do acquire by first exercising them, just as it happens in the arts. Anything that we have to learn to do we learn by the actual doing of it: people become builders by building and instrumentalists by playing instruments. Similarly we become just by performing just acts, brave by performing brave ones...like activities produce like dispositions. Hence we must give our activities a certain quality, because it is their characteristics that determine the resulting dispositions. So it is a matter of no little importance what sort of habits we form from the earliest age – it makes a vast difference, or rather all the difference in the world.[397]

—Aristotle

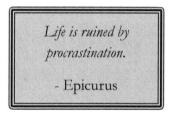

*Life is ruined by procrastination.*

- Epicurus

We are born once. We cannot be born a second time, and throughout eternity we shall of necessity no longer exist. You have no power over the morrow, and yet you put off your pleasure. Life is ruined by procrastination, and every one of us dies deep in his affairs.[398]
   —Epicurus

Remember how long you have procrastinated, and how consistently you have failed to put to good use your suspended sentence from the gods. It is about time you realized the nature of the universe (of which you are a part) and the power that rules it (to which your part owes its existence). Your days are numbered. Use them to throw open the windows of your soul to the sun. If you do not, the sun will soon set, and you with it.[399]
   —Marcus Aurelius

No carelessness in your actions. No confusion in your words. No imprecision in your thoughts. No retreating into your own soul, or trying to escape it. No overactivity.[400]
   —Marcus Aurelius

Whatever shall remain to be done virtue can do with courage and readiness. For anyone would admit that it is a mark of folly to do in a slothful and rebellious spirit whatever one has to do, or to direct the body in one direction and the mind in another, and thus to be torn between utterly conflicting emotions.[401]
   —Seneca

In a sense, people are our proper occupation. Our job is to do them good and put up with them. But when they obstruct our proper tasks, they become irrelevant to us – like sun, wind, animals. Our actions may be impeded by them, but there can be no impeding our intentions or our dispositions. Because we can accommodate and adapt. The mind adapts and converts to its own purposes the obstacles to our acting. The impediment to action advances action. What stands in the way becomes the way.[402]

   —Marcus Aurelius

For the originative cause of an action is the purpose for which it is done; but a person who is corrupted by pleasure or pain ceases at once to see that this is a cause at all: that is, he does not realize that he ought to make every choice as a means to that end, and perform every act on account of it; for vice tends to destroy the authority of the originative cause.[403]

   —Aristotle

When he was asked what he thought was the best occupation for a person, Socrates replied:
Effective action. I regard luck and action as totally opposed to each other. I consider that coming upon something that you need without looking for it is good luck, but to do a thing well after learning and practicing how to do it is, I think, effective action; and it is those who make a practice of this who seem to me to be effective.[404]

   —Socrates as quoted by Xenophon

Never act without purpose and resolve, or without the means to finish the job.[405]

   —Marcus Aurelius

Arm yourself for action with these two thoughts: first, do only what your sovereign and lawgiving reason tells you is for the good of others; and second, do not hesitate to change course if someone is able to show you where you are mistaken or point out a better way. Be persuaded only by arguments based on justice and the common good, never by what appeals to your taste for pleasure or popularity.[406]
—Marcus Aurelius

I don't complain about the lack of time...what little I have will go far enough. Today – this day – will achieve what no tomorrow will fail to speak about. I will lay siege to the gods and shake up the world.[407]
—Seneca

Do what nature demands. Get a move on – if you have it in you – and don't worry whether anyone will give you credit for it. And don't go expecting Plato's Republic; be satisfied with even the smallest progress, and treat the outcome of it all as unimportant.[408]
—Marcus Aurelius

There is nothing impossible to him who will try.[409]
—Alexander the Great

> *There is nothing impossible to him who will try.*
>
> - Alexander the Great

Well-being is realized by small steps, but is truly no small thing.[410]
—Zeno

Perfection is only attained by practice.[411]
—Plutarch

Tossing aside everything else, hold fast to these few truths. We
live only in the present, in this fleet-footed moment. The rest is
lost and behind us, or ahead of us and may never be found.[412]
—Marcus Aurelius

Build your life one action at a time, and be happy if each act you
perform contributes to a fulfilling and complete life. No one can
prevent you from doing this.
"But what if some outside circumstance stands in my way?"
Not even that can stop you from acting justly, wisely, and
reasonable.
"But it may block me from doing something I want to do."
Yes, but by welcoming the obstacle and by calmly adapting
your action to it, you will be able to do something else in harmony
with your goals and with the sort of life you are seeking to build.
Action by action.[413]
—Marcus Aurelius

If you don't have a consistent goal in life, you can't live in a consistent way...If you direct all your energies toward that, your actions
will be consistent. And so will you.[414]
—Marcus Aurelius

How long will you wait before you demand the best of yourself?...
If you remain careless and lazy, making excuse after excuse,
fixing one day after another when you will finally take yourself

in hand, your lack of progress will go unnoticed and in the end you will have lived and died unenlightened. Finally decide that you are an adult who is going to devote the rest of your life to making progress.[415]

—Epictetus

Don't act as though you'll live to be a thousand. Your days are numbered like everyone else's. In what remains of your allotted time, while you still can, become good.[416]

—Marcus Aurelius

There is indeed a limit fixed for us, just where the remorseless law of Fate has fixed it; but none of us knows how near he is to this limit. Therefore, let us so order our minds as if we had come to the very end. Let us postpone nothing. Let us balance life's account every day. The greatest flaw in life is that it is always imperfect, and that a certain part of it is postponed. One who daily puts the finishing touches to his life is never in want of time.[417]

—Seneca

It's not that we have a short time to live, but that we waste much of it. Life is long enough, and it's been given to us in generous measure for accomplishing the greatest things, if the whole of it is well invested. But when life is squandered through soft and careless living, and when it's spent on no worthwhile pursuit, death finally presses and we realize that the life which we didn't notice passing has passed away. So it is: the life we are given isn't short but we make it so; we're not ill provided but we are wasteful in life. Just as impressive and princely wealth is squandered in an instant when it passes into the hands of a poor manager, but wealth however modest grows through careful deployment if it is entrusted to a responsible guardian, just so our lifetime offers ample scope to the person who maps it out well.[418]

—Seneca

Make yourself believe the truth of my words, that certain moments are torn from us, that some are gently removed, and that others glide beyond our reach. The most disgraceful kind of loss, however, is that due to carelessness. Furthermore, if you will pay close heed to the problem, you will find that the largest portion of our life passes while we are doing ill, a goodly share while we are doing nothing, and the whole while we are doing that which is not to the purpose. What man can you show me who places any value on his time, who reckons the worth of each day, who understands that he is dying daily? For we are mistaken when we look forward to death; the major portion of death has already passed, whatever years be behind us are in death's hands. Therefore, Lucilius, do as you write me that you are doing: hold every hour in your grasp. Lay hold of today's task, and you will not need to depend so much upon tomorrow's. While we are postponing, life speeds by. Nothing, Lucilius, is ours, except time. We were entrusted by nature with the ownership of this single thing, so fleeting and slippery that anyone who will can oust us from possession. What fools these mortals be! They allow the cheapest and most useless things, which can easily be replaced, to be charged in the reckoning, after they have acquired them; but they never regard themselves as in debt when they have received some of that precious commodity, time! And yet time is the one loan which even a grateful recipient cannot repay.[419]

—Seneca

> *What man can you*
> *show me who places*
> *any value on his*
> *time, who reckons the*
> *worth of each day,*
> *who understands that*
> *he is dying daily?*
>
> - Seneca

Stop all this theorizing about what a good man should be. Be it![420]
—Marcus Aurelius

Those who are industrious conquer the greatest difficulties.[421]
—Plutarch

Every hour be firmly resolved...to accomplish the work at hand with fitting and unaffected dignity, goodwill, freedom, and justice. Banish from your thoughts all other considerations. This is possible if you perform each act as if it were your last, rejecting every frivolous distraction, every denial of the rule of reason, every pretentious gesture, vain show, and whining complaint against the decrees of fate. Do you see what little is required of a man to live a well-tempered and god-fearing life? Obey these precepts, and the gods will ask nothing more.[422]
—Marcus Aurelius

BOOK 9
# RESILIENCE

You are knocked down.

You get up.

You are knocked down, again.

You get up, again.

That is resilience. The ability to bounce back and show grit and grace despite whatever you are facing.

It is said that adversity reveals character, or as Epictetus notes, "the true man is revealed in difficult times." It is easy to be a positive leader when things are going well, but how do you respond when the tide has turned against you, when you suffer a setback, or when you fail completely either personally or professionally?

That is the true mark of a person's resilience, and you will find that what doesn't kill you makes you stronger.

The best things are the most difficult.[423]

—Plutarch

Purpose! Be assured that I shall not weaken mine.[424]

—Aeschylus

Life's no soft affair. It's a long road you've started on: you can't
but expect to have slips and knocks and falls...[425]

—Seneca

Cling tooth and nail to the following rule: not to give in to
adversity, never to trust prosperity, and always take full note of
fortune's habit of behaving just as she pleases.[426]

—Seneca

Above all things, respect yourself.[427]

—Pythagoras

To labor cheerfully and so endure
The wind that blows from heaven.[428]

—Marcus Aurelius

What does not hurt the community cannot hurt the individual.
Every time you think you've been wronged, apply this rule: if
the community isn't hurt by it, then neither am I. But what if the
community is hurt? Then don't be angry with the person who
caused the injury. Just help him to see his mistake.[429]

—Marcus Aurelius

Time teaches all things (Time brings all things to pass).[430]

—Aeschylus

A persevering steadfastness of purpose counts for a lot.[431]
—Seneca

To be like the rock that the waves keep crashing over. It stands
unmoved and the raging of the sea falls still around it.[432]
—Marcus Aurelius

> *To be like the rock that
> the waves keep crashing
> over. It stands unmoved
> and the raging of the
> sea falls still around it.*
>
> - Marcus Aurelius

A setback has often cleared the way for greater prosperity. Many
things have fallen only to rise to more exalted heights.[433]
—Seneca

Don't let your imagination be crushed by life as a whole.
Don't try to picture everything bad that could possibly happen. Stick with the situation at hand, and ask, "Why is this
so unbearable? Why can't I endure it?" You'll be embarrassed
by the answer.[434]
—Marcus Aurelius

The world is maintained by change.[435]
—Marcus Aurelius

By cosmic rule,
as day yields night,
so winter summer,
war peace, plenty famine.
All things change.
Fire penetrates the lump
of myrrh, until the joining
bodies die and rise again
in smoke called incense.[436]
—Heraclitus

For one thing is denied even to the gods:
To make what has been done undone again.[437]
—Agathon, as quoted by Aristotle

Ah! Miserable minds of men, blind hearts! In what darkness of life,
in what great dangers ye spend this little span of years...can you
doubt that all such power belongs to reason alone, above all when
the whole of life is but a struggle in darkness? For even as children
tremble and fear everything in blinding darkness, so we sometimes
dread in the light things that are no whit more to be feared than
what children shudder at in the dark, and imagine what will come
to pass. This terror then, this darkness of the mind, must be scat-
tered not by the rays of the sun and the gleaming shafts of day, but
by the outer view and the inner law of nature.[438]
—Lucretius

What doesn't transmit light creates its own darkness.[439]
—Marcus Aurelius

All things come from strife.[440]
—Heraclitus, as quoted by Aristotle

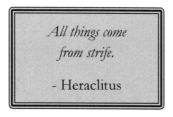

*All things come
from strife.*

- Heraclitus

Fire tests gold, misfortune brave men.[441]
—Seneca

But life is not worth living, and there is no limit to our sorrows, if we indulge our fears to the greatest possible extent; in this matter, let prudence help you, and contemn with a resolute spirit even when it is in plain sight. If you cannot do this, counter one weakness with another, and temper your fear with hope.[442]
—Seneca

It is tragic for the soul to be apprehensive of the future and wretched in anticipation of wretchedness, consumed with an anxious desire that the objects which give pleasure may remain in its possession to the very end. For such a soul will never be at rest; in waiting for the future it will lose the present blessings which it might enjoy. And there is no difference between grief for something lost and the fear of losing it.[443]
—Seneca

I judge you unfortunate because you have never lived through misfortune. You have passed through life without an opponent – no one can ever know what you are capable of, not even you yourself.[444]
—Seneca

Don't hope that events will turn out the way you want, welcome events in whichever way that they happen: this is the path to peace.[445]

—Epictetus

Whoever chafes at the conditions dealt by fate is unskilled in the art of life; whoever bears with them nobly and makes wise use of the results is a man who deserves to be considered good.[446]

—Epictetus

It's better to conquer grief than to deceive it.[447]

—Seneca

Dig deep within yourself, for there is a fountain of goodness ever ready to flow if you will keep digging.[448]

—Marcus Aurelius

Another person will not hurt you without your cooperation; you are hurt the moment you believe yourself to be.[449]

—Epictetus

> *Another person will not hurt you without your cooperation; you are hurt the moment you believe yourself to be.*
>
> - Epictetus

Choose not to be harmed – and you won't feel harmed. Don't feel harmed – and you haven't been.[450]
   —Marcus Aurelius

If you consider things outside your control as good or bad, then whenever something bad happens or something good fails to materialize, you blame the gods or are angry with men because they are, or could be, or someday might be responsible for the presence of some evil or the absence of some good. This sort of thinking breeds injustice. If, on the other hand, you think of only those things under your control as good or bad, then you will have no cause to find fault with God and no reason to quarrel with others.[451]
   —Marcus Aurelius

Someone wrongs me. Why should I care? That's his business—his inclinations and actions are up to him. I care only about what the universal nature wills for me, and I do what my own nature wills.[452]
   —Marcus Aurelius

You can bind up my leg, but not even Zeus has the power to break my freedom of choice.[453]
   —Epictetus

Anytus and Meletus can kill me, but cannot harm me.[454]
   —Socrates, as quoted by Epictetus

Hecato says, 'cease to hope and you will cease to fear.'...The chief cause of both these ills is that we do not adapt ourselves to the present, but send our thoughts a long way ahead. And so foresight, the noblest blessing of the human race, becomes perverted.[455]
   —Seneca

What else is freedom but the power to live our life the way we want?

'Nothing.'

Do you want to live life doing wrong?

'No.'

Therefore, no one doing wrong is free. Do you want to live your life in fear, grief and anxiety?

'Of course not.'

So no one in a state of constant fear is free either. By the same token, whoever has gained relief from grief, fear and anxiety has gained freedom.[456]

—Epictetus

Hope is the only good thing common to all men; those who have nothing else possess hope still.[457]

—Thales

And when a man is in the grip of difficulties he should say:
There may be pleasure in the memory
    Of Even these events one day.
    He should put his whole heart into the fight against them. If he gives way before them he will lose the battle; if he exerts himself against them he will win. What in fact most people do is pull down on their own heads what they should be holding up against; when something is in imminent danger of falling on you, the pressure of it bearing heavily on you, it will only move after you and become an even greater weight to support if you back away from it; if instead you stand your ground, willing yourself to resist, it will be forced back. Look at the amount of punishment that boxers and wrestlers take to the face and body generally! They will put up none the less with any suffering in their desire for fame, and will undergo it all not merely in the

course of fighting but in preparing for their fights as well: their training in itself constitutes suffering. Let us too overcome all things, with our reward consisting not in any wreath or garland, not in trumpet-calls for silence for the ceremonial proclamation of our name, but in moral worth, in strength of spirit, in a peace that is won for ever once in any contest fortune has been utterly defeated.[458]

—Seneca

Whenever you suffer pain, keep this thought handy: pain is nothing to be ashamed of, nor can it impair your mind, at least not the mind's ability to reason and to fulfill its social obligations. In most cases the words of Epicurus will help you: "Pain is never unbearable or unending, so long as you are mindful of its limits and bridle your imagination." [459]

—Marcus Aurelius

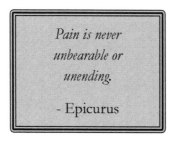

*Pain is never unbearable or unending.*

- Epicurus

Pain too is just a scary mask: look under it and you will see. The body sometimes suffers, but relief is never far behind. And if that isn't good enough for you, the door stands open; otherwise put up with it.[460]

—Epictetus

Pain is the price the gods require us to pay for all our benefits.[461]

—Epicharmus, as quoted by Socrates

It is easy for someone whose foot remains unsnared by suffering to give advice and criticize another in distress.[462]

—Aeschylus

Misfortune has a way of choosing some unprecedented means or other of impressing its power on those who might be said to have forgotten it...Terror strikes amid the most tranquil surroundings, and without any disturbance in the background to give rise to them calamities spring from the least expected quarter. States which stood firm through civil war as well as wars external collapse without a hand being raised against them. How few nations have made of their prosperity a lasting thing! This is why we need to envisage every possibility and to strengthen the spirit to deal with the things which may conceivably come about. Rehearse them in your mind: exile, torture, war, shipwreck. Misfortune may snatch you away from your country, or your country away from you, may banish you into some wilderness – these very surroundings in which the masses suffocate may become a wilderness. All the terms of our human lot should be before our eyes; we should be anticipating not merely all that commonly happens but all that is conceivably capable of happening, if we do not want to be overwhelmed and struck numb by rare events as if they were unprecedented ones; fortune needs envisaging in a thoroughly comprehensive way.[463]

—Seneca

In the middle of peace war rears its head, and the bulwarks of one's security are transformed into sources of alarm, friend turning foe and ally turning enemy. The summer's calm is upset by sudden storms more severe than those of winter. In the absence of any enemy we suffer all that an enemy might wreak on us.[464]

—Seneca

Perseverance is more prevailing than violence; and that many things which cannot be overcome when they are together, yield themselves up when taken little by little.[465]

—Sertorius, as quoted by Plutarch

> *Many things which cannot be overcome when they are together, yield themselves up when taken little by little.*
>
> - Sertorius

We ought, therefore, to bring ourselves to believe that all the vices of the crowd are, not hateful, but ridiculous, and to imitate Democritus rather than Heraclitus. For the latter, whenever he went forth into public, used to weep, the former to laugh; to the one all human doings seemed to be miseries, to the other follies. And so we ought to adopt a lighter view of things, and put up with them in an indulgent spirit; it is more human to laugh at life than to lament over it. Add, too, that he deserves better of the human race also who laughs at it than he who bemoans it; for the one allows it some measure of good hope, while the other foolishly weeps over things that he despairs of seeing corrected.[466]

—Seneca

You must stop blaming God, and not blame any person. You must completely control your desire and shift your avoidance to what lies within your reasoned choice. You must no longer feel anger, resentment, envy, or regret.[467]

　—Epictetus

The best revenge is not to do as they do.[468]

　—Marcus Aurelius

For nothing outside my reasoned choice can hinder or harm it – my reasoned choice alone can do this to itself. If we would lean this way whenever we fail, and would blame only ourselves and remember that nothing but opinion is the cause of a troubled mind and uneasiness, then by God, I swear we would be making progress.[469]

　—Epictetus

The mark and attitude of the philosopher: look for help and harm exclusively from yourself. And the signs of a person making progress: he never criticizes, praises, blames or points the finger, or represents himself as knowing or amounting to anything. If he experiences frustration or disappointment, he points the finger at himself...he keeps an eye on himself as if he were his own enemy lying in ambush.[470]

　—Epictetus

It is stupid to say, 'Tell me what to do!" What should I tell you? It would be better to say, 'Make my mind adaptable to any circumstance.' Saying 'Tell me what to do' is like an illiterate saying, 'Tell me what to write whenever I'm presented with a name.' If I say 'John' and then someone else comes along and gives him 'Jane' instead of 'John' to write, what is going to happen? How is he going to write it? If you have learned your letters, though, you are ready for anything anyone dictates. If you are not prepared,

I don't know what I should tell you to do. Because there may be events that call for you to act differently – and what will you do or say then? So hold on to this general principle and you won't need specific advice.[471]

—Epictetus

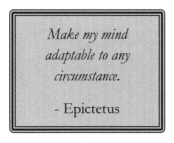

*Make my mind adaptable to any circumstance.*

- Epictetus

Easy tasks and momentary pleasures cannot produce physical fitness, as the experts in physical education remind us, or develop in the mind any knowledge worth mentioning; sustained application, however, enables us to achieve truly good results... Hesiod says somewhere:

Evil can be easily found, and freely;
Smooth is the road, and very near she swells.
But a sweat the gods have set upon the way
To goodness: long and steep is the path to it
And rough at first; but if you reach the summit
Thereafter it is easy, hard though it was.[472]

—Socrates

We must try to make the latter part of the journey better than the first, so long as we are en route; and when we reach the end, we must keep an even keel and remain cheerful.[473]

—Epicurus

No mortal goes through life unscathed,
free from pain until the end.
One trouble comes today,
yet another comes tomorrow.[474]
　　—Aeschylus

So in life our first job is this, to divide and distinguish things into two categories: externals I cannot control, but the choices I make with regard to them I do control. Where will I find good and bad? In me, in my choices. Don't ever speak of 'good' or 'bad,' 'advantage' or 'harm,' and so on, of anything that is not your responsibility.[475]
　　—Epictetus

It is when times are good that you should gird yourself for tougher times ahead, for when Fortune is kind the soul can build defenses against her ravages. So it is that soldiers practice maneuvers in peacetime, erecting bunkers with no enemies in sight and exhausting themselves under no attack so that when it comes they won't grow tired.[476]
　　—Seneca

The next time you are tempted to complain of your bad luck, remember to apply this maxim: "Bad luck borne nobly is good luck."[477]
　　—Marcus Aurelius

Success comes to the common man, and even to commonplace ability; but to triumph over the calamities and terrors of mortal life is the part of a great man only. Truly, to be always happy and to pass through life without mental pang is to be ignorant of one half of nature.[478]
　　—Seneca

Don't become disgusted with yourself, lose patience, or give up if you sometimes fail to act as your philosophy dictates, but after each setback, return to reason and be content if most of your acts are worthy of a good man.[479]

—Marcus Aurelius

How much better it is to heal than to avenge an injury! Vengeance consumes much time, and it exposes the doer to many injuries while he smarts from one; our anger always lasts longer than the hurt. How much better it is to take the opposite course and not to match fault with fault. Would anyone think that he was well balanced if he repaid a mule with kicks and a dog with biting?... If other creatures escape your anger for the very reason that they are lacking in understanding, every man who lacks understanding should hold in your eyes a like position.[480]

—Seneca

Nothing ever happens to a man that he is not equipped by nature to endure. Someone else experiences the same difficulty you have faced, and unaware of what has happened or not wanting to lose face, he remains undaunted and unharmed. Is it not shameful when ignorance and vanity outperform wisdom?[481]

—Marcus Aurelius

Remember, too, that the reason Athens has the greatest name in the world is because she has never given in to adversity.[482]

—Pericles

The wonderful efficacy and power of long and continuous labor you may see indeed every day in the world around you. Thus water continually dropping wears away rocks.[483]

—Plutarch

> *A rational being can turn each setback into raw material and use it to achieve its goal.*
>
> - Marcus Aurelius

We have various abilities, present in all rational creatures as in the nature of rationality itself. And this is one of them. Just as nature takes every obstacle, every impediment, and works around it – turns it to its purposes, incorporates it into itself – so, too, a rational being can turn each setback into raw material and use it to achieve its goal.[484]

—Marcus Aurelius

Remember, it is not enough to be hit or insulted to be harmed, you must believe that you are being harmed. If someone succeeds in provoking you, realize that your mind is complicit in this provocation. Which is why it is essential that we not respond impulsively to impressions; take a moment before reacting, and you will find it is easier to maintain control.[485]

—Epictetus

To love only what happens, what was destined. No greater harmony.[486]

—Marcus Aurelius

Don't be ashamed to ask for help. Take on life's tasks with the resolve of a soldier storming the breach. So what if you are lame and cannot scale the wall alone. Does your lameness prevent you from finding someone to help you?[487]

—Marcus Aurelius

The true man is revealed in difficult times. So when trouble comes, think of yourself as a wrestler whom God, like a trainer, has paired with a tough young buck. For what purpose? To turn you into Olympic-class material. But this is going to take some sweat to accomplish. From my perspective, no one's difficulties ever gave him a better test than yours, if you are prepared to make use of them the way a wrestler makes use of an opponent in peak condition.[488]

—Epictetus

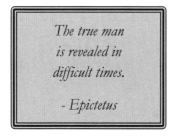

*The true man is revealed in difficult times.*

*- Epictetus*

He who learns must suffer. And even in our sleep, pain that cannot forget falls drop by drop upon the heart, and in our own despite, against our will, comes wisdom to us by the awful grace of God.[489]

—Aeschylus

BOOK 10

# WISDOM

What is wisdom?

Wisdom is a journey – one in which you can continue to make life-long strides but never quite reach the finish line.

Wisdom is not so much about knowing exactly what the answer is in a given situation, but more about equipping yourself to recognize particular circumstances or developments so you know how best to respond in the moment.

The main challenge with wisdom is that the primary method of gaining it is through experience, which means you will succeed but also likely fail countless times along the way.

But you can help yourself by seeking wisdom from the hard lessons learned from all those who came before you. Let their wisdom inform your own and you will be better equipped as a leader to face the myriad challenges in front of you.

Wisdom begins in wonder.[490]
  —Socrates

Wisdom is knowledge.[491]
  —Socrates

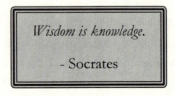

Of all the words yet spoken,
none come quite as far as wisdom,
which is the action of the mind
beyond all things that may be said.
Wisdom is the oneness
of mind that guides
and permeates all things.[492]
    —Heraclitus

The unexamined life is not worth living.[493]
    —Socrates

Know thyself.[494]
    —Inscription at the Oracle of Delphi

The man who does not understand the nature of the universe cannot know his place in it. Nor can he know who he is or what the universe is without understanding the purpose of the universe. Failing to understand these two things, he cannot begin to say why he was born.[495]
    —Marcus Aurelius

And isn't this obvious that people derive most of their bene-fits from knowing themselves, and most of their misfortunes from being self-deceived? Those who know themselves know what is appropriate for them and can distinguish what they can and cannot do; and, by doing what they understand, they both supply their needs and enjoy success, while, by refraining from doing things that they don't understand, they avoid making mistakes and escape misfortune. Self-knowledge also enables them to assess others; and it is through their relations with others that they provide themselves with what is good and guard against what is bad for them. Those who do not know themselves and are totally deceived about their own abilities are in the same position whether they are dealing with other people or any other aspect of human affairs. They don't know what they want or what they are doing or what means they are using; and, through making gross mistakes about all these, they miss the good things and get into trouble. People who know what they are doing succeed in their activities and become famous and respected...But those who don't know what they are doing make bad choices and fail in whatever they attempt, and so not only suffer loss and retribution in respect of these actions, but damage their reputation in consequence, get laughed at, and live despised and unhonored.[496]

—Socrates

So when my days have passed noiselessly away, lowly may I die and full of years. On him does death lie heavily, who, but too well known to all, dies to himself unknown.[497]

—Seneca

Don't be ignorant of yourself, or make the usual mistake. Most people, when they are set upon looking into other people's affairs, never turn to examine themselves. Don't shirk this responsibility, but make a greater effort to take yourself seriously.[498]

—Socrates

To my mind, the man who doesn't know his own ability is ignorant of himself.[499]

—Euthydemus conversation with Socrates

For herein is the evil of ignorance, that he who is neither good nor wise is nevertheless satisfied with himself: he has no desire for that of which he feels no want.[500]

—Plato

There are two kinds of disease of the soul...vice and ignorance.[501]

—Socrates

Education and morals...make a good man, and the same qualities will make a good citizen or good ruler.[502]

—Aristotle

Every circumstance represents an opportunity.[503]

—Epictetus

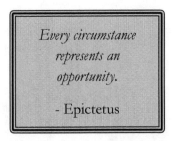

*Every circumstance represents an opportunity.*

- Epictetus

There is only one good, knowledge, and only one evil, ignorance.[504]

—Socrates

What does it mean to be getting an education? It means learning to apply natural preconceptions to particular cases as nature prescribes, and distinguishing what is in our power from what is not.[505]

—Epictetus

If you shape your life according to nature, you will never be poor; if according to people's opinions, you will never be rich.[506]

—Epicurus, as quoted by Seneca

A boxer derives the greatest advantage from his sparring partner.[507]

—Epictetus

You are doing the finest possible thing and acting in your best interests if...you are persevering in your efforts to acquire a sound understanding.[508]

—Seneca

To arrive at the truth is indeed the function of intellect in any aspect.[509]

—Aristotle

That man is best who sees the truth himself;
Good too is he who listens to wise counsel.
But who is neither wise himself nor willing
To ponder wisdom is not worth a straw.[510]

—Hesiod, as quoted by Aristotle

Whenever wisdom is present, good luck is redundant.[511]

—Socrates

The habit of knowledge
is not human but divine.[512]
    —Heraclitus

If a man objects to truths that are all too evident, it is no easy
task finding arguments that will change his mind. This is proof
neither of his own strength nor of his teacher's weakness. When
someone caught in an argument hardens to stone, there is just no
more reasoning with them.[513]
    —Epictetus

All people ought to know themselves
and everyone be wholly mindful.
To be even-minded
is the greatest virtue.
Wisdom is to speak
the truth and act
in keeping with its nature.[514]
    —Heraclitus

> *Wisdom is to speak*
> *the truth and act in*
> *keeping with its nature.*
>
> - Heraclitus

This alone is certain, that there is nothing certain.[515]
    —Pliny the Elder

Learn to bear the changes of fortune with magnanimity.[516]
    —Cleobulus

The forms of Virtue are justice, courage, temperance, magnificence, magnanimity, liberality, gentleness, prudence, wisdom.[517]
    —Aristotle

Leisure without study is death – a tomb for the living person.[518]
    —Seneca

Nature of any kind thrives on forward progress.[519]
    —Marcus Aurelius

How much more damage anger and grief do than the things that cause them.[520]
    —Marcus Aurelius

The essence of good and evil lies in an attitude of the will.[521]
    —Epictetus

I myself know nothing, except just a little, enough to extract an argument from another man who is wise and to receive it fairly.[522]
    —Socrates

Accept the prescriptions of nature as if they were intended for your own health, even if at times they may seem cruel or disagreeable to you. Remember that they are for the good of the universe and for the pleasure of God. Nothing is prescribed for any part that does not benefit the whole. After all, it would violate the nature of anything to act against its own interests in governing its parts. There are two reasons, then, for being content with whatever happens to you. The first is that it was meant just for you, prescribed for you, and preserved for you like a thread woven into your destiny from the very beginning. The second is that whatever happens to the individual contributes to the health, wholeness, and survival of the entire universe. You destroy the symmetry and continuity of the whole if you cut away even one part or remove a single cause. And that's what you do, to the extent you're able, every time you whine and complain—mutilate the whole by amputating the parts.[523]

—Marcus Aurelius

For surely *to be wise* is the most desirable thing in all the world. It is quite impossible to imagine anything better, or more becoming for a human being, or more appropriate to his essential nature. That is why the people who try to reach this goal are called philosophers, because that is precisely what philosophy means, the love of wisdom. And wisdom, according to the definition offered by early philosophers, signifies the knowledge of all things, divine and human, and of the causes which lie behind them. If anyone is prepared to disparage so noble a study as that, I cannot imagine anything he would find himself able to approve of![524]

—Cicero

Wisdom comes through suffering.
Trouble, with its memories of pain,
drips in our hearts as we try to sleep,
so men against their will
learn to practice moderation.
Favors come to us from gods
seated on their solemn thrones –
such grace is harsh and violent.[525]

—Aeschylus

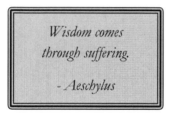

*Wisdom comes*
*through suffering.*

*- Aeschylus*

Withdraw into yourself, as far as you can. Associate with those who will make a better man of you. Welcome those whom you yourself can improve. The process is mutual; for men learn while they teach.[526]
—Seneca

For man, the best and most pleasant life is the life of the intellect, since the intellect is in the fullest sense of the man. So this life will also be the happiest...The man who exercises his intellect and cultivates it seems likely to be in the best state of mind and to be most loved by the gods.[527]
—Aristotle

Of all the things that wisdom provides for the happiness of the whole man, by far the most important is the acquisition of friendship. It is the same judgment that has made us feel confident that nothing fearful is of long duration or everlasting, and that has seen personal security during our limited span of life most nearly perfected by friendship.[528]
—Epicurus

The wise man, after adjusting himself to the bare necessities of life, understands better how to share than to take – so large is the fund of self-sufficiency that he has discovered.[529]
—Epicurus

Remind yourself that all men assert that wisdom is the greatest good, but that there are few who strenuously endeavor to obtain this greatest good.[530]

—Pythagoras

If anyone would take two words to heart and take pains to govern and watch over themselves by them, they will live an impeccable and immensely tranquil life. The two words are: persist and resist.[531]

—Epictetus, as related by Aulus Gellius

Pleasure induces us to behave badly, and pain to shrink from fine actions. Hence the importance (as Plato says) of having been trained in some way from infancy to feel joy and grief at the right things: true education is precisely this.[532]

—Aristotle

It is easy to praise providence for everything that happens in the world provided you have both the ability to see individual events in the context of the whole and a sense of gratitude. Without these, either you will not see the usefulness of what happens or, even supposing that you do see it, you will not be grateful for it.[533]

—Epictetus

There are three topics in philosophy, in which he who would be wise and good must be exercised: that of the desires and aversions, that he may not be disappointed of the one, nor incur the other; that of the pursuits and avoidances, and, in general, the duties of life, that he may act with order and consideration, and not carelessly; the third includes integrity of mind and prudence, and, in general, whatever belongs to the judgment. Of these points the principal and most urgent is that which reaches the passions; for passion is produced no otherwise than by a disappointment of one's desires and an incurring of one's aversions. It is this which introduces perturbations, tumults, misfortunes, and calamities; this is the spring of sorrow, lamentation, and envy; this renders us envious and emulous, and incapable of hearing reason.[534]

—Epictetus

Our ancestors had a custom, observed right down as far as my own lifetime, of adding to the opening words of a letter: 'I trust this finds you as it leaves me, in good health.' We have good reason to say: 'I trust this finds you in pursuit of wisdom.' For this is precisely what is meant by good health. Without wisdom the mind is sick, and the body itself, however physically powerful, can only have the kind of strength that is found in persons in a demented or delirious state. So this is the sort of healthiness you must make your principal concern.[535]

—Seneca

There is no need to suppose that human beings differ very much one from another: but it is true that the ones who come out on top are the ones who have been trained in the hardest school.[536]

—Thucydides

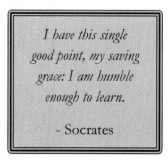

*I have this single good point, my saving grace: I am humble enough to learn.*

- Socrates

Do you see that I'm telling the truth, Hippias, when I say that I'm persistent in questioning clever people? This is probably my only good point: in other respects I'm pretty useless. I mean, I'm ignorant about the way things are, which just baffles me. I can easily prove this: whenever I meet anyone like you whose wisdom is famous and vouched for by all the Greeks, my ignorance becomes evident, because we disagree on almost everything. What greater proof of ignorance can there be than disagreement with experts? But, astonishingly, I have this single good point, my saving grace: I am humble enough to learn, so I probe and ask questions, and am extremely grateful to anyone who answers me. I always repay my debts by never passing the lesson off as a discovery of my own and so denying the fact that I have learned something.[537]

—Socrates

Give yourself the present. Those who chase after future fame fail to realize that the men whose praise they crave tomorrow will be no different from the men whose opinions they despise today, and all these men will die. What do you care whether tomorrow's men know the sound of your name or say nice things about you?[538]

—Marcus Aurelius

When a man goes out of his house, he should consider what he is going to do: and when he comes home again he should consider what he has done.[539]

—Cleobulus

Three of the greatest mistakes that can be made – lack of intelligence, lack of resolution, or lack of responsibility.[540]

—Thucydides

Opinions without knowledge are all ugly...Those who, without intelligence (understanding), have a true opinion are like blind men, going along on the right road.[541]

—Socrates

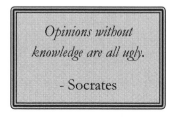

*Opinions without knowledge are all ugly.*

- Socrates

Surely this is the most objectionable kind of ignorance, to think one knows what one does not know.[542]

—Socrates

It is an attribute of man to have knowledge in another way besides those that we have described, because in the case of having knowledge without using it we can detect a different kind of having, so that a person can, in a sense, both have knowledge and not have it: e.g. if he is asleep or mentally disturbed or drunk. Now this is the condition of those who are in the grip of emotion; because quite obviously fits of temper and sexual craving and certain other such excitements actually produce physical changes, and in some cases even cause fits of madness.[543]

—Aristotle

We are responsible for some things, while there are others for which we cannot be held responsible. The former include our judgment, our impulse, our desire, aversion, and our mental faculties in general; the latter include the body, material possessions, our reputation, status – in a word, anything not in our power to control...Remember that if you mistake what is naturally inferior for what is sovereign and free, and what is not your business for your own, you'll meet with disappointment, grief and worry and be at odds with God and man. But if you have the right idea about what really belongs to you and what does not, you will never be subject to force or hindrance, you will never blame or criticize anyone, and everything you do will be done willingly. You won't have a single rival, no one to hurt you, because you will be proof against harm of any kind...So make a practice at once of saying to every strong impression: 'An impression is all you are, not the source of the impression.' Then test and assess it with your criteria, but one primarily: ask, 'is this something that is, or is not, in my control?' And if it's not one of the things that you control, be ready with the reaction, 'Then it's none of my concern.'[544]

—Epictetus

Whenever I see a person suffering from nervousness, I think, well, what can he expect? If he had not set his sights on things outside man's control, his nervousness would end at once...Just think: we aren't filled with fear except by things that are bad; and not by them, either, as long as it is in our power to avoid them. So, if externals are neither good nor bad, while everything within the sphere of choice is in our power and cannot be taken away by anyone, or imposed on us without our compliance —then what's left to be nervous about?[545]

—Epictetus

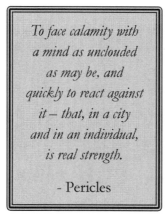

*To face calamity with a mind as unclouded as may be, and quickly to react against it — that, in a city and in an individual, is real strength.*

*- Pericles*

To face calamity with a mind as unclouded as may be, and quickly to react against it – that, in a city and in an individual, is real strength.[546]

—Pericles

The philosopher's goal: bring the will in line with events, so that nothing happens contrary to our wishes and, conversely, nothing fails to happen that we want to happen.[547]

—Epictetus

Trust no man as a friend till you have tried him.[548]

—Publius Syrus

I'll give you some rules to observe that will enable you to live in greater safety. You for your part I suggest should listen as carefully to the advice I give you as you would if I were advising you on how to look after your health...Now think of the things which goad man into destroying man: you'll find that they are hope, envy, hatred, fear and contempt. Contempt is the least important of the lot, so much so that a number of men have actually taken shelter behind it for protection's sake. For if a person feels contempt for someone, he tramples on him doubtless, but he passes on. No one pursues an unremitting and persistent policy of injury to a man for whom he feels nothing but contempt. Even in battle, the man on the ground is left alone, the fighting being with those still on their feet. Coming to hope, so long as you own nothing likely to arouse the greed or grasping instincts of others, so long as you possess nothing out of the ordinary (for people covet even the smallest things if they are rare or little known), you'll have nothing to worry about from the hopes of grasping characters. Envy you'll escape if you haven't obtruded yourself on other people's notice, if you haven't flaunted your possessions, if you've learnt to keep your satisfaction to yourself. Hatred either comes from giving offense, and that you'll avoid by refraining from deliberately provoking anyone, or is quite uncalled for: here your safeguard will be ordinary tact. It is a kind of hatred that has been a source of danger to a lot of people; men have been hated without having any actual enemy. As regards not being feared, a moderate fortune and an easy-going nature will secure you that. People should see that you're not a person it is dangerous to offend: and with you a reconciliation should be both easy and dependable. To be feared inside your own home, it may be added, is as much a source of trouble as being feared outside it – slave or free, there isn't a man who hasn't power enough to do you injury. Besides, to be feared is to fear: no one has been able to strike terror into others and at the same time enjoy peace of mind himself. There remains contempt. The person who has made contempt his ally, who has been despised because he has chosen to be despised, has the measure of it under his control. Its disadvantages are negatived by the possession of respected qualities and of friends having influence with some person with the necessary influence. Such influential friends are people with whom it is well worth having ties, without be-ing so tied up with them that their protection costs you more than the original danger might have done.[549]

—Seneca

To children who put their hand into a narrow jar and bring out figs and nuts...if they fill the hand, they cannot take it out, and then they cry. Drop a few of them and you will draw things out. And do you part with your desires: do not desire many things and you will have what you want.[550]

—Epictetus

Nothing should be called good that fails to enlarge our humanity. This excludes all those things that a man doesn't need in order to be human and that human nature doesn't fit him with or perfect in him. Whatever is excluded by this definition, then, has no bearing on man's purpose in life or on the good that sums up his purpose. Moreover, if any of the so-called good things our definition excludes were really essential to our humanity, why is it that doing without them or opposing them strengthens a man's reputation while showing moderation in their regard is considered "good?" The fact is, the more you free yourself from things of this sort and live happily without them, the more you will enlarge your humanity.[551]

—Marcus Aurelius

> *Nothing should be*
> *called good that fails to*
> *enlarge our humanity.*
>
> - Marcus Aurelius

So, if you become wise, my boy, everybody will be a friend to you, everybody will be close to you, since you'll be useful and good; but if you don't, neither your father nor your mother nor your close kin nor anyone else at all will be a friend to you.[552]

—Socrates conversation with Lysis

Remember the lessons of history. Remember how often whole peoples have allowed themselves to be persuaded to go to war by 'wise' men—and then been utterly destroyed by the very enemy they agreed to attack! Remember how many statesmen have helped raise new leadership to power—and then been overthrown by their own protégés! Remember how often leaders have chosen to treat their friends like slaves—and then perished in the revolutions caused by their idiotic methods! How many powerful men have craved to dominate the world—and by overreaching have lost everything they once possessed![553]

—Xenophon

But the wise person can lose nothing. Such a person has everything stored up for themselves, leaving nothing to Fortune, their own goods are held firm, bound in virtue, which requires nothing from chance, and therefore can't be either increased or diminished.[554]

—Seneca

It is essential for you to remember that the attention you give to any action should be in due proportion to its worth, for then you won't tire and give up, if you aren't busying yourself with lesser things beyond what should be allowed.[555]

—Marcus Aurelius

Always shun whatever may make you angry.[556]
 —Publius Syrus

No one can lead a happy life, or even one that is bearable, without the pursuit of wisdom, and that the perfection of wisdom is what makes the happy life, although even the beginnings of wisdom make life bearable. Yet this conviction, clear as it is, needs to be strengthened and given deeper roots through daily reflection; making noble resolutions is not as important as keeping the resolutions you have made already. You have to persevere and fortify your pertinacity until the will to good becomes a disposition to good.[557]
 —Seneca

The archer must know what he is seeking to hit; then he must aim and control the weapon by his skill. Our plans miscarry because they have no aim. When a man does not know what harbor he is making for, no wind is the right wind.[558]
 —Seneca

> *Our plans miscarry because they have no aim. When a man does not know what harbor he is making for, no wind is the right wind.*
>
> - Seneca

If you don't have a consistent goal in life, you can't live it in a consistent way. Unhelpful, unless you specify a goal...the goal should be a common one—a civic one. If you direct all your energies toward that, your actions will be consistent. And so will you.[559]

    —Marcus Aurelius

Don't ever forget these things:
    The nature of the world.
    My nature.
    How I relate to the world.
    What proportion of it I make up.
    That you are a part of nature, and no one can prevent you from speaking and acting in harmony with it always.[560]

    —Marcus Aurelius

What am I doing with my soul?
Interrogate yourself, to find out what inhabits your so-called mind and what kind of soul you have now.[561]

    —Marcus Aurelius

Applicants for wisdom
do what I have done:
inquire within.
Just as the river where I step
is not the same, and is,
so I am as I am not.[562]

    —Heraclitus

The human soul degrades itself:
    i.   Above all, when it does its best to become an abscess, a kind of detached growth on the world. To be disgruntled

at anything that happens is a kind of secession from Nature, which comprises the nature of all things.

ii. When it turns its back on another person or sets out to do it harm, as the souls of the angry do.

iii. When it is overpowered by pleasure or pain.

iv. When it puts on a mask and does or says something artificial or false.

v. When it allows its action and impulse to be without a purpose, to be random and disconnected: even the smallest things ought to be directed toward a goal. But the goal of rational beings is to follow the rule and law of the most ancient of communities and states.[563]

—Marcus Aurelius

This is the sort of person a truly wise man has to be. He will never do anything he might regret – or anything he does not want to do. Every action he performs will always be dignified, consistent, serious, upright. He will not succumb to the belief that this or that future event is predestined to happen; and no event, therefore, will cause him surprise, or strike him as unexpected or strange. Whatever comes up, he will continue to apply his own standards; and when he has made a decision, he will abide by it. A happier condition than that I am unable to conceive.

The belief of the Stoics on this subject is simple. The supreme good, according to them, is to live according to nature, and in harmony with nature. That, they declare, is the wise man's duty; and it is also something that lies within his own capacity to achieve. From this follows the deduction that the man who has the supreme good within his power also possesses the power to live happily. Consequently, the wise man's life is happy.[564]

—Cicero

Man's ideal state is realized when he has fulfilled the purpose for which he was born.[565]

—Seneca

> *Man's ideal state is realized when he has fulfilled the purpose for which he was born.*
>
> - Seneca

# ENDNOTES

1    Seneca the Younger, *Moral Letters to Lucilius*, trans. Richard Mott Gummere (London: Loeb, 1915), https://onemorelibrary.com/index.php/en/?option=com_djclassifieds&format=raw&view=download&task=download&fid=16913.

2    Qtd. in Fred Kofman, "Unconditional Responsibility: The Power of Being a Player," *Axialent Conscious Business*, accessed June 27, 2021, https://www.cu.edu/sites/default/files/Unconditional_Responsibility_by_Fred_Kofman.pdf.

3    Qtd. in Cora E. Lutz, "Musonius Rufus: 'The Roman Socrates,'" *Yale Classical Studies*, ed. Alfred Bellinger, vol. 10 (New Haven: Yale University Press, 1947), https://philocyclevl.files.wordpress.com/2016/09/yale-classical-studies-10-cora-e-lutz-ed-musonius-rufus_-the-roman-socrates-yale-university-press-1947.pdf.

4    Qtd. in Valerio Capraro and Alessandra Marcelleti, "Do Good Actions Inspire Good Actions in Others?", *Scientific Reports* 4, no. 7470 (December 2014), https://doi.org/10.1038/srep07470.

5    Epictetus, *Discourses and Selected Writings*, trans. and ed. Robert Dobbin (New York: Penguin Books, 2008), 81.

6    Qtd. in Kathleen Freeman, *Ancilla to Pre-Socratic Philosophers: A Complete Translation of the Fragments in Diels*, Fragmente Der Vorsokratiker (Cambridge, MA: Harvard University Press), 32.

7    Benjamin Beckhart, *Lead with Character: Build a Better Future* (self-pub., 2019), 79.

8    Xenophon, *Conversations of Socrates*, trans. Robin Waterfield (New York: Penguin Books, 1990), 76.

9    Marcus Aurelius, *The Emperor's Handbook*, trans. C. Scot Hicks and David Hicks (New York: Simon & Schuster, 2002), 55.

10 Seneca, *Letters from a Stoic*, trans. Robin Campbell (New York: Penguin Books, 2004), 39.

11 Aristotle, *Aristotle: The Complete Works, Politics* (n.p.: Pandora's Box, 2021), Kindle.

12 Aristotle, *The Nicomachean Ethics*, trans. J. A. K. Thomson (New York: Penguin Books, 2004), 167.

13 Epictetus, *Discourses and Selected Writings*, 112.

14 Plato, *Plato in Twelve Volumes*, vol. 1, *Crito*, sec. 48b, trans. Harold North Fowler (Cambridge, MA: Harvard University Press, 1966), accessed June 13, 2021, http://data.perseus.org/citations/urn:cts:greekLit:tlg0059.tlg003.perseus-eng1:48b.

15 Qtd. in "Foundation of Narrative Theory: Aristotle's *Poetics*," Columbia University, accessed August 7, 2020, http://www.columbia.edu/itc/hs/medical/cp2/film/client_edit/notes_2_27.html.

16 Qtd. in "Sparta: Famous Quotes about Spartan Life," *The Greeks: Crucible of Civilization*, PBS, accessed March 5, 2021, https://www.pbs.org/empires/thegreeks/background/8c_p1.html.

17 Marcus Aurelius, *The Emperor's Handbook*, 113.

18 Xenophon, *Conversations of Socrates*, 94.

19 Qtd. in Linda Elder and Richard Paul, *25 Days to Better Thinking and Better Living: A Guide for Improving Every Aspect of Your Life* (Upper Saddle River, NJ: FT Press, 2006), 33.

20 Aristotle, *The Nicomachean Ethics*, 61.

21 Epictetus, "Enchiridion," *Discourses and Selected Writings*, trans. and ed. Robert Dobbin (New York: Penguin Books, 2008), 239.

22 Marcus Aurelius, *The Emperor's Handbook*, 39.

23 Aristotle, *Aristotle: The Complete Works, Rhetoric*, (n.p.:Pandora's Box, 2021), Kindle.

24 Marcus Aurelius, *The Emperor's Handbook*, 91.

25 Aristotle, *The Nicomachean Ethics*, 62–63.

26 Marcus Aurelius, *The Emperor's Handbook*, 77.

27 Aristotle, *Poetics*, trans. S. H. Butcher, Project Gutenberg, accessed June 25, 2022, https://www.gutenberg.org/files/1974/1974-h/1974-h.htm.

28 Marcus Aurelius, *The Emperor's Handbook*, 79.

29 Aristotle, *The Nicomachean Ethics*, 31.

30 Epictetus, "Enchiridion," 227–228.

31 Marcus Aurelius, *The Emperor's Handbook*, 92.

32 Cicero, *On the Good Life*, trans. Michael Grant (New York: Penguin Books, 1971), 90.

33 Marcus Aurelius, *The Emperor's Handbook*, 139.

34 Marcus Aurelius, *The Emperor's Handbook*, 144.

35 Epictetus, *Discourses and Selected Writings*, 11.

36 Cicero, *On the Good Life*, 128.

37 Aeschylus, *Agamemnon*, trans. Ian Johnston, accessed July 27, 2021, http://johnstoniatexts.x10host.com/aeschylus/agamemnonhtml.html.

38 Xenophon, *Conversations of Socrates*, 127.

39 Thucydides, *How to Think about War: An Ancient Guide to Foreign Policy*, trans. Johanna Hanink (Princeton: Princeton University Press, 2019), 69–71.

40 Marcus Aurelius, *The Emperor's Handbook*, 71.

41 Epictetus, *Discourses and Selected Writings*, 47.

42 Epictetus, *Discourses and Selected Writings*, 69.

43 Seneca, *Letters from a Stoic*, 99.

44 Epictetus, *Discourses and Selected Writings*, 82.

45 Seneca, *Letters from a Stoic*, 36–37.

46 Epictetus, "Enchiridion," 225.

47 Seneca, *Letters from a Stoic*, 46.

48 Marcus Aurelius, *The Emperor's Handbook*, 99.

49 Seneca, *Letters from a Stoic*, 176–177.

50 Aristotle, *The Nicomachean Ethics*, 165.

51 Epictetus, *Discourses and Selected Writings*, 123.

52 Seneca, *Letters from a Stoic*, 56.

53 Aristotle, *The Nicomachean Ethics*, 24.

54 Seneca, *Letters from a Stoic*, 140.

55 Aristotle, *The Nicomachean Ethics*, 278.

56 Diogenes Laertius, *The Lives and Opinions of Eminent Philosophers*, trans. C. D. Yonge, Project Gutenberg, accessed September 23, 2021, https://www.gutenberg.org/files/57342/57342-h/57342-h.htm#Page_63.

57 Aristotle, *The Nicomachean Ethics*, 279.

58 Qtd. in Larry Hedrick, *Xenophon's Cyrus the Great: The Arts and Leadership of War*, (New York: St Martin's, 2006), Kindle, 273.

59 Xenophon, *Conversations of Socrates*, 215.

60 Lucretius, *On the Nature of Things*, trans. Ian Johnston, accessed July 30, 2021, http://johnstoniatexts.x10host.com/lucretius/lucretius3html.html.

61    Aristotle, *The Nicomachean Ethics*, 226.

62    Qtd. in Ryan Holiday and Stephen Hanselman, *The Daily Stoic: 366 Meditations on Wisdom, Perseverance, and The Art of Living* (New York: Portfolio/Penguin, 2016), 106.

63    Publius Syrus, *The Moral Sayings*, trans. Darius Lyman (Cleveland: L.E. Barnard & Company, 1856), 36.

64    Cicero, *De Officiis (On Duties)*, trans. Walter Miller, Tufts University, accessed May 15, 2022, http://www.perseus.tufts.edu/hopper/text?doc=Perseus%3Atext%3A2007.01.0048%3Abook%3D1%3Asection%3D141.

65    Epictetus, *Discourses and Selected Writings*, 151.

66    Marcus Aurelius, *Meditations*, trans. Gregory Hays (New York: Modern Library, 2002), 97.

67    Thucydides, *History of the Peloponnesian War*, trans. Rex Warner (New York: Penguin Books, 149.

68    Plato, "The Apology," *Great Dialogues of Plato*, trans. W. H. D. Rouse (New York: Signet Classic, 1999), 436.

69    Qtd. in Holiday and Hanselman, *The Daily Stoic*, 140.

70    Qtd. in Holiday and Hanselman, *The Daily Stoic*, 204.

71    Epictetus, *Discourses and Selected Writings*, 197.

72    Aristotle, *The Nicomachean Ethics*, 245.

73    Thucydides, *History of the Peloponnesian War*, 159–160.

74    Seneca, *Letters from a Stoic*, 76.

75    Qtd. in Holiday and Hanselman, *The Daily Stoic*, 199.

76    Qtd. in Hedrick, *Xenophon's Cyrus the Great*, 22.

77    Publius Syrus, *The Moral Sayings*, 20.

78    Qtd. in Holiday and Hanselman, *The Daily Stoic*, 362.

79    Qtd. in Holiday and Hanselman, *The Daily Stoic*, 202.

80    Marcus Aurelius, *Meditations*, 69.

81    Qtd. in Justin Tyme, *Ultimate Organization Leadership: 225 Tips from Socrates, Aristotle, and Alexander the Great* (n.p., 2012), Kindle.

82    Pliny the Elder, *Letters of Pliny*, trans. William Melmoth, Project Gutenberg, accessed November 4, 2021, http://www.gutenberg.org/files/2811/2811-h/2811-h.htm#link2H_4_0065.

83    Thucydides, *How to Think about War*, 49.

84    Aristotle, *The Nicomachean Ethics*, 66.

85    Seneca, *Letters from a Stoic*, 194.

86  Homer, *The Iliad*, University of Baltimore, accessed April 10, 2022, https://home.ubalt.edu/ntygfit/ai 01 pursuing fame/ai 01 tell/iliad06.htm.

87  Thucydides, *History of the Peloponnesian War*, 159.

88  Homer, *The Iliad*, trans. Samuel Butler, Project Gutenberg, accessed July 23, 2022, https://www.gutenberg.org/files/2199/2199-h/2199-h.htm.

89  Plato, "The Apology," 434.

90  Aristotle, *The Nicomachean Ethics*, 34.

91  Marcus Aurelius, *Meditations*, 92.

92  Xenophon, *Conversations of Socrates*, 43.

93  Publius Syrus, *The Moral Sayings*, 53.

94  Qtd. in Fred T. Jane, *The British Battle Fleet: Its Inception and Growth Throughout the Centuries to the Present Day* (London: The Library Press, 1915), 106–107.

95  Marcus Aurelius, *The Emperor's Handbook*, 65.

96  Qtd. in Hedrick, *Xenophon's Cyrus the Great*, 35.

97  *Plutarch's Lives*, vol. 1, ed. Aubrey Stewart and George Long (London: George Bell and Sons, 1906), 443.

98  Publius Syrus, *The Moral Sayings*, 997.

99  Qtd. in William Ebenstein and Alan Ebenstein, *Great Political Thinkers: Plato to the Present*, 6th ed. (Belmont: Wadsmorth, 2000), 163.

100  Seneca the Younger, *Moral Letters to Lucilius*.

101  Aristotle, *The Nicomachean Ethics*, 73.

102  Publius Syrus, *The Moral Sayings*, 35.

103  Seneca, *Letters from a Stoic*, 191.

104  Thucydides, *History of the Peloponnesian War*, 85.

105  Aristotle, *The Nicomachean Ethics*, 67–68.

106  Thucydides, *History of the Peloponnesian War*, 149–150.

107  Plato, "The Apology," 444.

108  Homer, *The Iliad*, trans. Edward, Earl of Derby, Project Guttenberg, accessed July 20, 2022, https://www.gutenberg.org/files/6150/6150-h/6150-h.htm#linknoteref-4:~:text=And%20if%20there%20be%20among%20you%2C,His%20heritage%20uninjur'd.

109  Qtd. in Holiday and Hanselman, *The Daily Stoic*, 193.

110  Thucydides, *History of the Peloponnesian War*, 161.

111  Marcus Aurelius, *The Emperor's Handbook*, 35.

112  Seneca, *Letters from a Stoic*, 81.

113  Xenophon, *Conversations of Socrates*, 60–161.

114 Thucydides, *History of the Peloponnesian War*, 180–181.

115 Seneca, *Letters from a Stoic*, 199.

116 Xenophon, *Conversations of Socrates*, 304.

117 Thucydides, *History of the Peloponnesian War*, 123.

118 Aristotle, *The Nicomachean Ethics*, 35.

119 Thucydides, *How to Think about War*, 67.

120 Epictetus, *Discourses and Selected Writings*, 78.

121 Marcus Aurelius, *The Emperor's Handbook*, 78.

122 Marcus Aurelius, *The Emperor's Handbook*, 104.

123 Arrian, *The Anabasis of Alexander*, translated by E. J. Chinnock, Project Gutenberg, accessed July 26, 2022, https://www.gutenberg.org/files/46976/46976-h/46976-h.htm.

124 Qtd. in Henry Kissinger, *Address by Secretary of State Kissinger*, accessed April 7, 2022, https://history.state.gov/historicaldocuments/frus1969-76v38p1/d71.

125 Epictetus, "Enchiridion," 243.

126 Marcus Aurelius, *The Emperor's Handbook*, 72.

127 Marcus Aurelius, *The Emperor's Handbook*, 80–81.

128 Cicero, *On the Good Life*, 141.

129 Seneca, *On the Happy Life*, accessed August 9, 2021, https://trisagionseraph.tripod.com/Texts/Happy.html.

130 Marcus Aurelius, *Meditations*, 103.

131 Marcus Aurelius, *The Emperor's Handbook*, 127.

132 Aristotle, *The Nicomachean Ethics*, 226.

133 Marcus Aurelius, *The Emperor's Handbook*, 27.

134 Epictetus, *Discourses and Selected Writings*, 45–46.

135 Marcus Aurelius, *The Emperor's Handbook*, 87.

136 Publius Syrus, *The Moral Sayings*, 65.

137 Marcus Aurelius, *The Emperor's Handbook*, 65.

138 Thucydides, *History of the Peloponnesian War*, 61.

139 Marcus Aurelius, *The Emperor's Handbook*, 75.

140 Qtd. in Hedrick, *Xenophon's Cyrus the Great*, 254.

141 Marcus Aurelius, *Meditations*, 154.

142 Aristotle, *The Nicomachean Ethics*, 101.

143 Marcus Aurelius, *The Emperor's Handbook*, 75.

144 Marcus Aurelius, *The Emperor's Handbook*, 93.

145 Boris Johnson, "Athenian Civilization: The Glory that Endures," Legatum Institute, accessed July 13, 2021, https://lif.blob.core.windows.net/

lif/docs/default-source/default-library/athenian-civilisation---the-glo-ry-that-endures-boris-johnson-(roads-to-freedom-series-legatum-institute)-4-september-2014.pdf?sfvrsn=0.

146 Marcus Aurelius, *The Emperor's Handbook*, 114.

147 Seneca the Younger, *Moral Letters to Lucilius*.

148 Marcus Aurelius, *The Emperor's Handbook*, 82.

149 Cicero, *De Officiis (On Duties)*.

150 Marcus Aurelius, *Meditations*, 151.

151 Marcus Aurelius, *Meditations*, 154.

152 Seneca the Younger, *Moral Letters to Lucilius*.

153 Aristotle, *The Nicomachean Ethics*, 249.

154 Marcus Aurelius, *The Emperor's Handbook*. 47.

155 Thucydides, *How to Think about War*, 81–83.

156 Qtd. in Holiday and Hanselman, *The Daily Stoic*, 214.

157 Epictetus, *Discourses and Selected Writings*, 211.

158 Marcus Aurelius, *The Emperor's Handbook*, 81.

159 Epictetus, "Enchiridion," 240.

160 Qtd. in Holiday and Hanselman, *The Daily Stoic*, 159.

161 Cicero, *De Finibus*, University of Chicago, accessed May 14, 2021, https://penelope.uchicago.edu/Thayer/E/Roman/Texts/Cicero/de_Finibus/5*.html.

162 Qtd. in Hedrick, *Xenophon's Cyrus the Great*, 29.

163 Marcus Aurelius, *The Emperor's Handbook*, 97.

164 Seneca the Younger, *Moral Letters to Lucilius*.

165 Publius Syrus, *The Moral Sayings*, 14.

166 Thucydides, *How to Think about War*, 91.

167 Qtd. in Holiday and Hanselman, *The Daily Stoic*, 84.

168 Qtd. in Holiday and Hanselman, *The Daily Stoic*, 257.

169 Qtd. in Holiday and Hanselman, *The Daily Stoic*, 258.

170 Qtd. in Holiday and Hanselman, *The Daily Stoic*, 297.

171 Seneca the Younger, *Moral Letters to Lucilius*.

172 Epictetus, *Discourses and Selected Writings*, 46.

173 Plato, *Gorgias*, trans. Benjamin Jowett, Project Gutenberg, accessed January 9, 2022, https://www.gutenberg.org/files/1672/1672-h/1672-h.htm.

174 Epictetus, *Discourses and Selected Writings*, 133–134.

175 Marcus Aurelius, *The Emperor's Handbook*, 120.

176 Cicero, *On the Good Life*, 221.

177  Qtd. in Holiday and Hanselman, *The Daily Stoic*, 216.

178  Seneca, *Letters from a Stoic*, 157.

179  Epictetus, "Enchiridion," 231.

180  Qtd. in Hedrick, *Xenophon's Cyrus the Great*, 13.

181  Marcus Aurelius, *The Emperor's Handbook*, 47.

182  Cicero, *On the Good Life*, 129–130.

183  Marcus Aurelius, *The Emperor's Handbook*, 144.

184  Qtd. in Holiday and Hanselman, *The Daily Stoic*, 222.

185  Marcus Aurelius, *The Emperor's Handbook*, 92–93.

186  Cicero, *On the Good Life*, 227.

187  Seneca, *On Tranquility of Mind*, accessed July 13, 2022, https://trisagion-seraph.tripod.com/Texts/Tranquility.html.

188  Marcus Aurelius, *Meditations*, 73–74.

189  Epictetus, *Discourses and Selected Writings*, 117.

190  Plutarch, *Morals*, trans. Arthur Richard Shilleto, Project Gutenberg, accessed July 28, 2022, https://www.gutenberg.org/files/23639/23639-h/23639-h.htm#Page_1.

191  Seneca, *Letters from a Stoic*, 34.

192  Thucydides, *How to Think about War*, 51.

193  Marcus Aurelius, *The Emperor's Handbook*, 81.

194  Qtd. in Hedrick, *Xenophon's Cyrus the Great*, 40.

195  Qtd. in Holiday and Hanselman, *The Daily Stoic*, 109.

196  Qtd. in Hedrick, *Xenophon's Cyrus the Great*, 245.

197  Seneca, *Letters from a Stoic*, 182.

198  Qtd. in Edith Hamilton, *The Greek Way* (New York: W.W. Norton & Company Inc., 2017), 135.

199  Aristotle, *The Nicomachean Ethics*, 139.

200  Aristotle, *Aristotle: The Complete Works, Nicomachean Ethics*, (n.p.: Pandora's Box), Kindle.

201  Qtd. in Strohmeier and Westbrook, *Divine Harmony: The Life and Teachings of Pythagoras*, (Rockville: Harmonia Books, 2012), 139.

202  Qtd. in Ratcliffe, ed., *Oxford Essential Quotations 5th Edition*, Oxford Reference, accessed April 15, 2022, https://www.oxfordreference.com/view/10.1093/acref/9780191826719.001.0001/q-oro-ed4-00010264.

203  Marcus Aurelius, *The Emperor's Handbook*, 104.

204  Aristotle, *The Nicomachean Ethics*, 32.

205  Epicurus, *The Art of Happiness*, trans. George K. Strodach (New York: Penguin Books, 2012), 175.

206 Publius Syrus, *The Moral Sayings*, 13.

207 Qtd. in Ebenstein and Ebenstein, *Great Political Thinkers*, 163.

208 Aristotle, *The Nicomachean Ethics*, 142.

209 Marcus Aurelius, *Meditations,* 118.

210 Plato, *Great Dialogues of Plato, The Republic,* trans. W. H. D. Rouse (New York: Signet Classic, 1999), 408.

211 Epicurus, *The Art of Happiness,* 178.

212 Marcus Aurelius, *The Emperor's Handbook,* 126.

213 Aristotle, *The Nicomachean Ethics*, 202.

214 Diogenes Laertius, *The Lives and Opinions of Eminent Philosophers.*

215 Aristotle, *The Nicomachean Ethics*, 48.

216 Diogenes Laertius, *The Lives and Opinions of Eminent Philosophers.*

217 Marcus Aurelius, *The Emperor's Handbook*, 140.

218 Cicero, *On the Good Life*, 345–346.

219 Cicero, *De Legibus (Treatise on the Laws)*, trans. Francis Barham, Online Library of Liberty, accessed August 6, 2021, https://oll.libertyfund.org/title/cicero-treatise-on-the-laws.

220 Aristotle, *Aristotle: The Complete Works, Politics.*

221 Marcus Aurelius, *The Emperor's Handbook*, 42.

222 Cicero, *On the Good Life*, 137.

223 Aristotle, *The Nicomachean Ethics*, 138.

224 Marcus Aurelius, *The Emperor's Handbook*, 43.

225 Cicero, *On the Good Life*, 137.

226 Marcus Aurelius, *The Emperor's Handbook*, 103.

227 Cicero, *On the Good Life*, 139.

228 Cicero, *On the Good Life*, 141.

229 Aristotle, *The Nicomachean Ethics*, 115.

230 Epicurus, *The Art of Happiness*, 173.

231 Epicurus, *The Art of Happiness,* 66.

232 Qtd. in Herbert Weir Smyth, *Aeschylus, Fragment 209,* Internet Archive, accessed July 15, 2021, https://archive.org/stream/aeschyluswitheng02aescuoft#page/496/mode/2up.

233 Marcus Aurelius, *The Emperor's Handbook,* 74.

234 Thucydides, *History of the Peloponnesian War,* 76.

235 Marcus Aurelius, *Meditations,* 161.

236 Publius Syrus, *The Moral Sayings*, 14.

237 Marcus Aurelius, *The Emperor's Handbook,* 140.

238 Thucydides, *History of the Peloponnesian War,* 80.

239 Marcus Aurelius, *The Emperor's Handbook*, 117.

240 Thucydides, *On Justice, Power, and Human Nature: Selections from The History of the Peloponnesian War*, trans. Paul Woodruff (Indianapolis: Hackett Publishing Company, 1993), 18.

241 Heraclitus, *Fragments*, trans. Brooks Haxton (New York: Penguin Books, 2001), 81.

242 Marcus Aurelius, *The Emperor's Handbook*, 81.

243 Marcus Aurelius, *The Emperor's Handbook*, 114.

244 Thucydides, *History of the Peloponnesian War*, 159.

245 Diogenes Laertius, *The Lives and Opinions of Eminent Philosophers*.

246 Marcus Aurelius, *The Emperor's Handbook*, 96.

247 Epictetus, "Enchiridion," 238.

248 Pseudo-Callisthenes, *The Romance of Alexander the Great*, trans. Albert Mugrdich Wolohojian (New York: Columbia University Press, 1969), http://www.attalus.org/armenian/Tales_Alexander_Wolohojian_trans.pdf.

249 Diogenes Laertius, *The Lives and Opinions of Eminent Philosophers*.

250 Epictetus, *Discourses and Selected Writings*, 102.

251 Diogenes Laertius, *The Lives and Opinions of Eminent Philosophers*.

252 Diogenes Laertius, *The Lives and Opinions of Eminent Philosophers*.

253 Marcus Aurelius, *Meditations*, 81.

254 Seneca, *Thyestes*, trans. Frank Justus Miller, Theoi Classical Texts Library, accessed September 15, 2021, https://www.theoi.com/Text/SenecaThyestes.html.

255 Qtd. in Thomas Benfield Harbottle, *Dictionary of Quotations (Classical)* (New York: The MacMillan Company, 1897), 455.

256 Qtd. in Tyron Edwards, *A Dictionary of Thoughts: Being a Cyclopedia of Laconic Quotations from the Best Authors of the World, both Ancient and Modern* (New York: Cassell Publishing Company, 1908), 525.

257 Thucydides, *History of the Peloponnesian War*, 47.

258 Heraclitus, *Fragments*, 5–7.

259 Publius Syrus, *The Moral Sayings*, 79.

260 Qtd. in Hedrick, *Xenophon's Cyrus the Great*, 109.

261 Cicero, *On the Good Life*, 287.

262 Cicero, *On the Good Life*, 287.

263 Qtd. in Robert O. Wray Jr., *Saltwater Leadership: A Primer on Leadership for the Junior Sea-Service Officer*, (Annapolis: Naval Institute Press, 2013), 41.

264 Xenophon, *Conversations of Socrates*, 197.

265 Seneca the Younger, *Moral Letters to Lucilius.*

266 Publius Syrus, *The Moral Sayings*, 79.

267 Aristotle, *The Nicomachean Ethics*, 105–106.

268 Qtd. in Strohmeier and Westbrook, *Divine Harmony: The Life and Teachings of Pythagoras*, 140.

269 Qtd. in Holiday and Hanselman, *The Daily Stoic*, 118.

270 Epictetus, *Discourses*, trans. Thomas Wentworth Higginson, Tufts University, accessed September 13, 2021, http://www.perseus.tufts.edu/hopper/text?doc=Perseus%3Atext%3A1999.01.0237%3Atext%3Ddisc%3Abook%3D3%3Achapter%3D18.

271 Publius Syrus, *The Moral Sayings*, 86.

272 Plutarch, *The Parallel Lives: The Life of Cato the Younger* (London: Loeb, 1919), accessed August 5, 2021, http://penelope.uchicago.edu/Thayer/E/Roman/Texts/Plutarch/Lives/Cato_Minor*.html.

273 Seneca, *Letters from a Stoic*, 84–85.

274 Epictetus, "Enchiridion," 236.

275 Seneca, *Letters from a Stoic*, 212.

276 Qtd. in Hamilton, *The Greek Way*, 74.

277 Qtd. in Ratcliffe, ed., *Oxford Essential Quotations 5th Edition*, Oxford Reference, accessed April 15, 2022, https://www.oxfordreference.com/view/10.1093/acref/9780191843730.001.0001/q-oro-ed5-00005519.

278 Qtd. in Ratcliffe, ed., *Oxford Essential Quotations 5th Edition*, Oxford Reference, accessed June 2, 2022, https://www.oxfordreference.com/view/10.1093/acref/9780191843730.001.0001/q-oro-ed5-00000159.

279 Qtd. in Wray Jr., *Saltwater Leadership*, 130.

280 Marcus Aurelius, *Meditations*, 147.

281 Qtd. in Hedrick, *Xenophon's Cyrus the Great*, 29.

282 Seneca, *On Tranquility of Mind.*

283 Marcus Aurelius, *The Emperor's Handbook*, 101.

284 Seneca, *Letters from a Stoic*, 33.

285 Marcus Aurelius, *The Emperor's Handbook*, 102.

286 Qtd. in Holiday and Hanselman, *The Daily Stoic*, 15.

287 Marcus Aurelius, *The Emperor's Handbook*, 46.

288 Steven Stavropoulos, *The Beginning of All Wisdom: Timeless Advice from the Ancient Greeks* (New York: Marlowe & Company, 2003), 48.

289 Seneca the Younger, *Moral Letters to Lucilius.*

290 Qtd. in Holiday and Hanselman, *The Daily Stoic*, 283.

291 Publius Syrus, *The Moral Sayings*, Maxim 8, translated by Darius Lyman, (Cleveland: L.E. Barnard & Company, 1856), p. 13.

292 Thucydides, *How to Think about War*, 131–133.

293 Qtd. in Holiday and Hanselman, *The Daily Stoic*, 162.

294 Qtd. in Holiday and Hanselman, *The Daily Stoic*, 332.

295 Marcus Aurelius, *Meditations*, 78.

296 Stewart and Long, *Plutarch's Lives*, 399.

297 Marcus Aurelius, *Meditations*, 93.

298 Epictetus, *Discourses and Selected Writings*, 95.

299 Heraclitus, *Fragments*, 9.

300 Aristotle, *Aristotle: The Complete Works, On the Soul* (n.p.: Pandora's Box), Kindle.

301 Qtd. in Holiday and Hanselman, *The Daily Stoic*, 336.

302 Qtd. in Diogenes Laertius, *The Lives and Opinions of Eminent Philosophers*.

303 Marcus Aurelius, *The Emperor's Handbook*, 29.

304 Epictetus, *Discourses and Selected Writings*, 201.

305 Epictetus, "Enchiridion," 232.

306 Qtd. in Holiday and Hanselman, *The Daily Stoic*, 308.

307 Aristotle, *The Nicomachean Ethics*, 146.

308 Marcus Aurelius, *The Emperor's Handbook*, 93.

309 Marcus Aurelius, *The Emperor's Handbook*, 129.

310 Marcus Aurelius, *The Emperor's Handbook*, 141.

311 Marcus Aurelius, *The Emperor's Handbook*, 123.

312 Epictetus, *Discourses and Selected Writings*, 203.

313 Epictetus, "Enchiridion," 223.

314 Epictetus, *Discourses and Selected Writings*, 47.

315 Xenophon, *Conversations of Socrates*, 205.

316 Epictetus, "Enchiridion," 223.

317 Marcus Aurelius, *Meditations*, 59.

318 Epictetus, *Discourses and Selected Writings*, 146.

319 Seneca, *Letters from a Stoic*, 61.

320 Marcus Aurelius, *The Emperor's Handbook*, 34.

321 Epictetus, *Discourses and Selected Writings*, 110.

322 Epictetus, *Discourses and Selected Writings*, 64.

323 Marcus Aurelius, *The Emperor's Handbook*, 41.

324 Xenophon, *Conversations of Socrates*, 172.

325 Epictetus, *Discourses and Selected Writings*, 153.

326 Seneca, *Letters from a Stoic*, 35.

327  Seneca, *Letters from a Stoic*, 196.

328  Thucydides, *How to Think about War*, 53.

329  Xenophon, *Conversations of Socrates*, 74.

330  Marcus Aurelius, *The Emperor's Handbook*, 48.

331  Epicurus, *The Art of Happiness*, 176–177.

332  Epictetus, *Discourses and Selected Writings*, 13.

333  Epicurus, *The Art of Happiness*, 182.

334  Marcus Aurelius, *The Emperor's Handbook*, 100.

335  Plato, *Early Socratic Dialogues*, trans. Donald Watt (New York: Penguin Books, 2005), 195.

336  Marcus Aurelius, *The Emperor's Handbook*, 105.

337  Plato, *Phaedrus*, trans. Benjamin Jowett, The Internet Classics Archive, accessed August 13, 2021, http://classics.mit.edu/Plato/phaedrus.html.

338  Epicurus, *The Art of Happiness*, 177.

339  Marcus Aurelius, *The Emperor's Handbook*, 37.

340  Xenophon, *The Memorable Things of Socrates*, trans. Edward Bysshe, (Dublin: George Faulkner, 1747), p. 318.

341  Marcus Aurelius, *The Emperor's Handbook*, 94.

342  Epictetus, *Discourses and Selected Writings*, 203.

343  Marcus Aurelius, *The Emperor's Handbook*, 42.

344  Heraclitus, *Fragments*, 31–33.

345  Aristotle, *The Nicomachean Ethics*, 270.

346  Marcus Aurelius, *Meditations*, 119.

347  Marcus Aurelius, *The Emperor's Handbook*, 75.

348  Marcus Aurelius, *Meditations*, 86.

349  Marcus Aurelius, *The Emperor's Handbook*, 107.

350  Qtd. in Strohmeier and Westbrook, *Divine Harmony*, 140.

351  Marcus Aurelius, *The Emperor's Handbook*, 38.

352  Seneca, *Letters from a Stoic*, 178.

353  Qtd. in Holiday and Hanselman, *The Daily Stoic*, 348.

354  Cicero, *De Officiis (On Duties)*.

355  Qtd. in Holiday and Hanselman, *The Daily Stoic*, 213.

356  Thucydides, *History of the Peloponnesian War*, 74.

357  Qtd. in Hedrick, *Xenophon's Cyrus the Great*, 5.

358  Marcus Aurelius, *The Emperor's Handbook*, 29.

359  Aeschylus, *Prometheus Bound*, trans. Ian Johnston, Universidade de São Paulo, accessed May 15, 2022, https://edisciplinas.usp.br/pluginfile.php/2596054/

mod_resource/content/1/PROMETHEUS%20BOUND%20BY%20 AESCHYLLUS.pdf.

360 Marcus Aurelius, *The Emperor's Handbook*, 91.

361 Thucydides, *History of the Peloponnesian War*, 147.

362 Heraclitus, *Fragments*, 73.

363 Aristotle, *The Nicomachean Ethics*, 33.

364 Marcus Aurelius, *The Emperor's Handbook*, 141.

365 Cicero, *On the Good Life*, 354.

366 Cicero, *On the Good Life*, 344.

367 Aristotle, *Aristotle: The Complete Works, On the Soul*.

368 Epictetus, *Discourses and Selected Writings*, 168.

369 Aristotle, *The Nicomachean Ethics*, 146.

370 Marcus Aurelius, *Meditations*, 30.

371 Arrian, *The Anabasis of Alexander*.

372 Xenophon, *Conversations of Socrates*, 107.

373 Qtd. in Holiday and Hanselman, *The Daily Stoic*, 143.

374 Aeschylus, *Prometheus Bound*.

375 Xenophon, *Conversations of Socrates*, 82.

376 Seneca the Younger, *Moral Letters to Lucilius*.

377 Qtd. in Oliver J. Thatcher, *The Ideas That Have Influenced Civilization in the Original Documents: Plutarch* (Milwaukee: The Roberts-Manchester Publishing Co., 1901), 389.

378 Marcus Aurelius, *Meditations*, 19.

379 Publius Syrus, *The Moral Sayings*, 55.

380 Publius Syrus, *The Moral Sayings*, 56.

381 Heraclitus, *Fragments*, 83.

382 Seneca the Younger, *Moral Letters to Lucilius*.

383 Qtd. in Holiday and Hanselman, *The Daily Stoic*, 13.

384 Marcus Aurelius, *Meditations*, 65.

385 Epictetus, *Discourses*, trans. Thomas Wentworth Higginson, Tufts University, accessed September 15, 2021, http://www.perseus.tufts.edu/ hopper/text?doc=Perseus%3Atext%3A1999.01.0236%3Atext%3Ddis-c%3Abook%3D2%3Achapter%3D18.

386 Qtd. in Wray Jr., *Saltwater Leadership*, 137.

387 Epictetus, "Enchiridion," 242.

388 Plato, *Cratylus*, trans. Harold Fowler, Tufts University, accessed April 4, 2022, http://www.perseus.tufts.edu/hopper/text?doc=Perseus%3Atex-t%3A1999.01.0172%3Atext%3DCrat.%3Asection%3D401d.

389 Thucydides, *How to Think about War*, 53.

390 Xenophon, *The Memorabilia*, Project Gutenberg, accessed July 30, 2021, https://www.gutenberg.org/files/1177/1177-h/1177-h.htm#link2H_4_0004.

391 Marcus Aurelius, *Meditations*, 53.

392 Aristotle, *The Nicomachean Ethics*, 19.

393 Marcus Aurelius, *The Emperor's Handbook*, 75.

394 Aristotle, *The Nicomachean Ethics*, 48.

395 Epictetus, "Enchiridion," 238.

396 Marcus Aurelius, *The Emperor's Handbook*, 109.

397 Aristotle, *The Nicomachean Ethics*, 32.

398 Epicurus, *The Art of Happiness*, 181.

399 Marcus Aurelius, *The Emperor's Handbook*, 28.

400 Marcus Aurelius, *Meditations*, 112.

401 Seneca the Younger, *Moral Letters to Lucilius*.

402 Marcus Aurelius, *Meditations*, 60.

403 Aristotle, *The Nicomachean Ethics*, 151.

404 Xenophon, *Conversations of Socrates*, 163.

405 Marcus Aurelius, *The Emperor's Handbook*, 41.

406 Marcus Aurelius, *The Emperor's Handbook*, 44.

407 Qtd. in Holiday and Hanselman, *The Daily Stoic*, 156.

408 Marcus Aurelius, *Meditations*, 124.

409 Qtd. in Orison Swett Marden, *Pushing to the Front, or, Success under Difficulties: A Book of Inspiration* (Bexar: Bibliotech Press, 1896), 55.

410 Qtd. in Holiday and Hanselman, *The Daily Stoic*, 161.

411 Plutarch, *Morals*.

412 Marcus Aurelius, *The Emperor's Handbook*, 37.

413 Marcus Aurelius, *The Emperor's Handbook*, 96–97.

414 Marcus Aurelius, *Meditations*, 155–156.

415 Epictetus, "Enchiridion," 244.

416 Marcus Aurelius, *The Emperor's Handbook*, 44.

417 Seneca the Younger, *Moral Letters to Lucilius*.

418 Seneca, *On the Shortness of Life*, trans. Gareth Williams, Internet Archive, accessed May 10, 2022, https://archive.org/stream/SenecaOnTheShortnessOfLife/Seneca+on+the+Shortness+of+Life_djvu.txt.

419 Seneca, *Epistles*, trans. Richard M. Gummere, Stoics, accessed June 14, 2021, https://www.stoics.com/seneca_epistles_book_1.html#'I1.

420 Marcus Aurelius, *The Emperor's Handbook*, 118.

421 Plutarch, *Morals*.

422 Marcus Aurelius, *The Emperor's Handbook*, 28.

423 Plutarch, *Morals*.

424 Aeschylus, *Agamemnon*, trans. Herbert Weir Smyth, Harvard University Center for Hellenic Studies, accessed July 25, 2022, https://chs.harvard.edu/primary-source/aeschylus-agamemnon-sb/.

425 Seneca, *Letters from a Stoic*, 197.

426 Seneca, *Letters from a Stoic*, 139.

427 Qtd. in Strohmeier and Westbrook, *Divine Harmony*, 139.

428 Marcus Aurelius, *Meditations*, 93.

429 Marcus Aurelius, *The Emperor's Handbook*, 60.

430 Aeschylus, *Prometheus Bound*.

431 Seneca, *Letters from a Stoic*, 107.

432 Marcus Aurelius, *Meditations*, 48.

433 Seneca, *Letters from a Stoic*, 181.

434 Marcus Aurelius, *Meditations*, 108.

435 Marcus Aurelius, *Meditations*, 18.

436 Heraclitus, *Fragments*, 25.

437 Aristotle, *The Nicomachean Ethics*, 147.

438 Titus Lucretius Carus, *On the Nature of Things*, trans. Cyril Bailey, Online Library of Liberty, accessed June 6, 2022, https://oll.libertyfund.org/title/bailey-on-the-nature-of-things.

439 Marcus Aurelius, *Meditations*, 113.

440 Aristotle, *The Nicomachean Ethics*, 202.

441 Seneca, *De Providentia*, trans. John Basore, Loeb Classical Library, accessed November 25, 2021, https://www.loebclassics.com/search?source=%2Fseneca younger-de providentia%2F1928%2Fwork.xml&sourceType=teipage&q=fire.

442 Seneca the Younger, *Moral Letters to Lucilius*.

443 Seneca the Younger, *Moral Letters to Lucilius*.

444 Seneca, *On Providence*, Tufts University, accessed July 14, 2021, http://www.perseus.tufts.edu/hopper/text?doc=Perseus%3Atext%3A2007.01.0012%3Abook%3D1%3Achapter%3D4%3Asection%3D3.

445 Epictetus, "Enchiridion," 224.

446 Epictetus, *Discourses and Selected Writings*, 210.

447 Seneca, *On Consolation to Helvia*, trans. John W. Basore, Tufts University, accessed July 27, 2022, http://www.perseus.tufts.edu/hopper/text?doc=Perseus%3Atext%3A2007.01.0017%3Abook%3D11%3Achapter%3D17%3Asection%3D1.

448 Qtd. in Holiday and Hanselman, *The Daily Stoic*, 317.

449 Epictetus, "Enchiridion," 234.

450 Marcus Aurelius, *Meditations*, 39.

451 Marcus Aurelius, *The Emperor's Handbook*, 73.

452 Marcus Aurelius, *The Emperor's Handbook*, 60.

453 Qtd. in Holiday and Hanselman, *The Daily Stoic*, 268.

454 Epictetus, *Discourses and Selected Writings*, 82.

455 Seneca the Younger, *Moral Letters to Lucilius*.

456 Epictetus, *Discourses and Selected Writings*, 79.

457 Qtd. in Edwards, *A Dictionary of Thoughts*, 234.

458 Seneca, *Letters from a Stoic*, 135–136.

459 Marcus Aurelius, *The Emperor's Handbook*, 87.

460 Epictetus, *Discourses and Selected Writings*, 79.

461 Xenophon, *Conversations of Socrates*, 105.

462 Aeschylus, *Prometheus Bound*.

463 Seneca, *Letters from a Stoic*, 179–180.

464 Seneca, *Letters from a Stoic*, 178.

465 Plutarch, *Parallel Lives: Sertorius*, trans. John Dryden, Internet Classics Archive, accessed June 25, 2022, http://classics.mit.edu/Plutarch/sertoriu.html.

466 Seneca, *On Tranquility of Mind*.

467 Qtd. in Holiday and Hanselman, *The Daily Stoic*, 233.

468 Marcus Aurelius, *The Emperor's Handbook*, 65.

469 Qtd. in Holiday and Hanselman, *The Daily Stoic*, 246.

470 Epictetus, "Enchiridion," 242–243.

471 Epictetus, *Discourses and Selected Writings*, 83.

472 Xenophon, *Conversations of Socrates*, 105.

473 Epicurus, *The Art of Happiness*, 182.

474 Aeschylus, *Libation Bearers*, trans. Ian Johnston, Fænum Publishing, accessed July 5, 2022, http://www.faenumpublishing.com/uploads/2/3/9/8/23987979/aeschylus_libation_bearers_a_dual_language_edition_-_johnston.pdf.

475 Epictetus, *Discourses and Selected Writings*, 86.

476 Qtd. in Holiday and Hanselman, *The Daily Stoic*, 272.

477 Marcus Aurelius, *The Emperor's Handbook*, 51.

478  Seneca, *Moral Essays: On Providence.*

479  Marcus Aurelius, *The Emperor's Handbook*, 56.

480  Seneca, *Moral Essays: On Anger*, trans. John W. Basore, Loeb Classical Library, accessed July 13, 2021, https://www.stoics.com/seneca_essays_book_1.html#ANGER1.

481  Marcus Aurelius, *The Emperor's Handbook*, 59.

482  Thucydides, *History of the Peloponnesian War*, 162.

483  Plutarch, *Morals.*

484  Marcus Aurelius, *Meditations*, 108.

485  Epictetus, "Enchiridion," 228–229.

486  Marcus Aurelius, *Meditations*, 94.

487  Marcus Aurelius, *The Emperor's Handbook*, 78.

488  Epictetus, *Discourses and Selected Writings*, 56.

489  Qtd. in Hamilton, *The Greek Way*, 61.

490  Qtd. in Hamilton, *The Greek Way*, 124.

491  Xenophon, *Conversations of Socrates*, 208.

492  Heraclitus, *Fragments*, 13.

493  Epictetus, *Discourses and Selected Writings*, 63.

494  Qtd. in Hamilton, *The Greek Way*, 31.

495  Marcus Aurelius, *The Emperor's Handbook*, 101.

496  Xenophon, *Conversations of Socrates*, 186–187.

497  Seneca, *Thyestes.*

498  Xenophon, *Conversations of Socrates*, 157–158.

499  Xenophon, *Conversations of Socrates*, 186.

500  Plato, *The Symposium*, The Internet Classics Archive, accessed June 25, 2021, http://classics.mit.edu/Plato/symposium.html.

501  Plato, *Sophist*, trans. Benjamin Jowett, The Internet Classics Archive, accessed July 7, 2022, http://classics.mit.edu/Plato/sophist.1b.txt.

502  Aristotle, *Politics*, trans. William Ellis, Project Gutenberg, accessed July 20, 2022, https://www.gutenberg.org/files/6762/6762-h/6762-h.htm.

503  Epictetus, *Discourses and Selected Writings*, 155.

504  Diogenes Laertius, *The Lives and Opinions of Eminent Philosophers.*

505  Epictetus, *Discourses and Selected Writings*, 54.

506  Seneca, *Letters from a Stoic*, 65.

507  Epictetus, *Discourses and Selected Writings*, 155.

508  Seneca, *Letters from a Stoic*, 86.

509  Aristotle, *The Nicomachean Ethics*, 146.

510  Aristotle, *The Nicomachean Ethics*, 8.

511  Plato, *Early Socratic Dialogues*, 329.

512  Heraclitus, *Fragments*, 63.

513  Epictetus, *Discourses and Selected Writings*, 15.

514  Heraclitus, *Fragments*, 71.

515  Pliny the Elder, *The Natural History*, trans. John Bostock and H. T. Riley, Tufts University, accessed October 15, 2021, http://www.perseus.tufts.edu/hopper/text?doc=Perseus%3Atext%3A1999.02.0137%3Abook%3D2%3Achapter%3D5.

516  Diogenes Laertius, *The Lives and Opinions of Eminent Philosophers*.

517  Aristotle, *Aristotle: The Complete Works, On the Soul*.

518  Qtd. in Holiday and Hanselman, *The Daily Stoic*, 288.

519  Marcus Aurelius, *Meditations*, 102.

520  Marcus Aurelius, *Meditations*, 153.

521  Qtd. in Ebenstein and Ebenstein, *Great Political Thinkers*, 154.

522  Socrates, *Theaetetus*, trans. Harold N. Fowler, Tufts University, accessed March 24, 2021, http://www.perseus.tufts.edu/hopper/text?doc=Perseus%3Atext%3A1999.01.0172%3Atext%3DTheaet.%3Asection%3D161b.

523  Marcus Aurelius, *The Emperor's Handbook*, 56.

524  Cicero, *On the Good Life*, 121.

525  Aeschylus, *Agamemnon*, translated by Ian Johnston.

526  Seneca, *Letters from a Stoic*, 43.

527  Aristotle, *The Nicomachean Ethics*, 272–276.

528  Epicurus, *The Art of Happiness*, 177–178.

529  Epicurus, *The Art of Happiness*, 182.

530  Qtd. in Thomas Taylor, *Life of Pythagoras* (London: A.J. Valpy Publishing, 1818), 261.

531  Qtd. in Holiday and Hanselman, *The Daily Stoic*, 303.

532  Aristotle, *The Nicomachean Ethics*, 35.

533  Epictetus, *Discourses and Selected Writings*, 16.

534  Epictetus, *Discourses*, trans. Thomas Wentworth Higginson, Tufts University, accessed July 31, 2022, http://www.perseus.tufts.edu/hopper/text?doc=Perseus%3Atext%3A1999.01.0237%3Atext%3Ddisc%3Abook%3D3%3Achapter%3D2.

535  Seneca, *Letters from a Stoic*, 60.

536  Thucydides, *History of the Peloponnesian War*, 85.

537  Plato, *Early Socratic Dialogues*, 286.

538  Marcus Aurelius, *The Emperor's Handbook*, 99.

539 Diogenes Laertius, *The Lives and Opinions of Eminent Philosophers*.

540 Thucydides, *History of the Peloponnesian War*, 106.

541 Plato, *Great Dialogues of Plato, The Republic*, 305.

542 Plato, *Great Dialogues of Plato, The Republic*, 435.

543 Aristotle, *The Nicomachean Ethics*, 174.

544 Epictetus, "Enchiridion," 221–222.

545 Epictetus, *Discourses and Selected Writings*, 103–104.

546 Thucydides, *History of the Peloponnesian War*, 162–163.

547 Epictetus, *Discourses and Selected Writings*, 107.

548 Publius Syrus, *The Moral Sayings*, 22.

549 Seneca, *Letters from a Stoic*, 195–196.

550 Epictetus, *Discourses*, The Internet Classics Archive, accessed July 30, 2021, http://classics.mit.edu/Epictetus/discourses.3.three.html.

551 Marcus Aurelius, *The Emperor's Handbook*, 58.

552 Plato, *Early Socratic Dialogues*, 140.

553 Qtd. in Hedrick, *Xenophon's Cyrus the Great*, 28.

554 Qtd. in Holiday and Hanselman, *The Daily Stoic*, 295.

555 Qtd. in Holiday and Hanselman, *The Daily Stoic*, 251.

556 Publius Syrus, *The Moral Sayings*, 73.

557 Seneca, *Letters from a Stoic*, 63.

558 Seneca the Younger, *Moral Letters to Lucilius*.

559 Marcus Aurelius, *Meditations*, 155–156.

560 Marcus Aurelius, *Meditations*, 19.

561 Marcus Aurelius, *Meditations*, 58.

562 Heraclitus, *Fragments*, 51.

563 Marcus Aurelius, *Meditations*, 22.

564 Cicero, *On the Good Life*, 95–96.

565 Seneca, *Letters from a Stoic*, 88.

Made in United States
Troutdale, OR
11/02/2023

14250567R00123